THE ART OF PERSUASION

STEWARD LA CASCE AND

TERRY BELANGER

THE ART OF PERSUASION:

HOW TO WRITE EFFECTIVELY ABOUT ALMOST ANYTHING

CHARLES SCRIBNER'S SONS
NEW YORK

A-3.72 [C]

Printed in the United States of America
Library of Congress Catalog Card Number 78-38278
SBN 684-12861-6 (Trade cloth)
SBN 684-12833-0 (Trade paper, SL)

Acknowledgements

Grateful acknowledgment is made to the following authors, pub-
lishers, agents, and individuals for their permission to reprint material in this anthology:

CYRILLY ABELS. For Paul Jacobs, "The Most Cheerful Graveyard in
the World," in *Reporter* (September 18, 1958), pp. 26–30.

GEORGE ALLEN & UNWIN LTD. For British and Canadian rights for
Bertrand Russell, *Unpopular Essays*, p. 149.

APPLETON-CENTURY-CROFTS. For Albert C. Baugh, *A History of the
English Language*, 2nd ed., © 1957, p. 300.

EDWARD ARNOLD LTD. For world rights (except U.S.) for E. M.
Forster, "What I Believe,' in *Two Cheers for Democracy*, p. 76.

ATLANTIC MONTHLY. For Gen. David M. Shoup, "The New American Militarism" (April 1969), p. 53, col. 1. Copyright © 1969 by
The Atlantic Monthly Company, Boston, Mass.

BASIL BLACKWELL. For world rights (except U.S.) for Hugh Sykes
Davies, "Irony and the English Tongue," in Brian Vickers, ed., *The
World of Jonathan Swift*, p. 144.

THE BOBBS-MERRILL COMPANY, INC. For Philip Wheelwright, *A Critical Introduction to Ethics*, 3rd ed., 1959, Chapter 1.

JONATHAN CAPE LTD. For rights in the British Commonwealth and
Empire for Eldridge Cleaver, *Soul on Ice*. For world rights (except
U.S.) for Percy Lubbock, *The Craft of Fiction*, p. 112.

MARCHETTE CHUTE. For "Getting at Truth," in *Saturday Review*
(September 19, 1953), pp. 11, 27.

HENRY STEELE COMMAGER. For "The University as Employment
Agency," in *The New Republic* (February 24, 1968), p. 26.

CORNELL UNIVERSITY PRESS. For Marjorie Hope Nicolson, *Mountain
Gloom and Mountain Glory: The Development of the Aesthetics of
the Infinite.* © 1959 by Cornell University, p. 35.

DAEDALUS. For Bruno Bettleheim, "The Problem of Generations."
Reprinted by permission of *Daedalus*, Journal of the American
Academy of Arts and Sciences, Boston, Mass. (Winter 1962) *Youth:
Change and Challenge*, p. 88.

HAROLD MATSON COMPANY INC. For Eric Sevareid, *The American Dream*, © 1968, (originally published in *Look*, July 9, 1968).

ROLLO MAY. For "Antidotes for the New Puritanism," *Saturday Review* (March 26, 1966), p. 42.

JULLIAN MESSNER. For Jacob Bronowski, *Science and Human Values*, © 1965, p. 6.

WILLIAM MORROW & CO., INC. For rights (except United Kingdom and Commonwealth) for LeRoi Jones, *Home: Social Essays by LeRoi Jones*, from "City of Harlem," 1962, 1966 by LeRoi Jones.

NATIONAL REVIEW. For Max Geltman, "The New Left and the Old Right," *National Review* (June 13, 1967), p. 632.

JACK NEWFIELD. For "A Populist Manifesto: The Making of a New Majority," in *New York Magazine* (July 19, 1971), p. 46, cols. 2–3.

THE NEW REPUBLIC. For "Support Your Local Police," (June 21, 1969), p. 9.

NEW YORK MAGAZINE. For Jack Newfield, "A Populist Manifesto: The Making of a New Majority." *New York* (July 19, 1971), p. 46.

THE NEW YORK REVIEW OF BOOKS. For Jonathan Miller, "TV Guide," (October 7, 1971), p. 29.

THE NEW YORK TIMES. For Lewis Feuer, "Should College Students Grade Their Teachers? The Risk is 'Juvenocracy,'" p. 56, col. 4, p. 57, col. 1 of the *New York Times* Magazine (September 18, 1966). For Alfred Kazin, "Literature as a Necessity of Life," in the *New York Times* Book Review, p. 4, (July 30, 1967). For James Baldwin, "The American Dream and the American Negro," *New York Times* Magazine, p. 33 (March 7, 1965).

NORTHWESTERN UNIVERSITY PRESS. For J. H. Hexter, *Reappraisals in History*, © 1961, from "Personal Retrospect and Postscript." For Arie J. Haagen-Smit, "The Troubled Outdoors," in *Interactions of Man and his Environment*, ed. Burgess H. Jennings and John E. Murphy, © 1966 by Northwestern University, p. 48.

W. W. NORTON & CO., INC. For Edith Hamilton, *The Greek Way*, Norton Library Edition, © 1964, from "The Idea of Tragedy," p. 138.

OXFORD UNIVERSITY PRESS. For *Pope and his Contemporaries: Essays Presented to George Sherburn*, ed. James L. Clifford and Louis A. Landa, © 1949 by the Clarendon Press, Oxford, from Louis I. Bredvold's "The Gloom of the Tory Satirists."

LAURENCE POLLINGER LIMITED. For rights in the British Commonwealth (except Canada) for William H. Whyte, Jr., *The Organization Man* (Jonathan Cape Ltd.), pp. 14–22.

DAVID RIESMAN. For David Riesman, "Where Is the College Generation Headed?" from *Atlantic Monthly* (April 1961).

THE SATURDAY REVIEW. For Marchette Chute, "Getting at Truth" (September 19, 1953), p. 11. For Rollo May, "Antidotes for the New Puritanism," (March 26, 1966), p. 42. For Norman Cousins, "All Hail Andy Barker," (August 8, 1970), p. 26. For Goodman Ace, "Top of My Head: The Finger, Having Writ, Starts Running," (August 29, 1970), p. 4.

SCIENCE. For Norbert Wiener, "Some Moral and Technical Consequences of Automation" (May 6, 1960), Vol. 131, pp. 1355–1358.

MARTIN SECKER & WARBURG LTD. For British Empire rights for Lewis Mumford, *The Highway and the City*.

SIMON & SCHUSTER, INC. For rights in the United States and Canada for William H. Whyte, Jr., *The Organization Man*, pp. 14–22. For rights in the United States for Bertrand Russell, *Unpopular Essays*, p. 149. For Max Lerner, *America as a Civilization: Life and Thought in the United States Today* © 1957, pp. 82–83.

VIKING PRESS INC. For rights (except the British Commonwealth) for John Steinbeck, *Travels with Charley*, © 1961, 1962 by the Curtis Publishing Co., Inc., © 1962 by John Steinbeck, p. 21. For rights in the United States for Percy Lubbock, *The Craft of Fiction*, © 1954, 1955, p. 112.

BARBARA WARD. For Barbara Ward, "Hindsight and Foresight in the World's Economy," p. 26, *Columbia Forum* (Spring 1969).

YALE UNIVERSITY PRESS. For James L. Clifford, "A Biographer Looks at Dr. Johnson," p. 131 of *New Light on Dr. Johnson*, F. W. Hilles, ed. For Allen T. Hazen, "The Earlier Owners of Horace Walpole's Books," p. 169 in *Horace Walpole: Writer, Politician, and Connoisseur*, © 1967.

PREFACE

Aristotle defined rhetoric as "the faculty of discovering the means of persuasion in reference to any subject whatever." *The Art of Persuasion* is an analysis of these means as they apply to any form of prose writing. The first two chapters concern ways of organizing arguments. The next three concern methods of influencing a reader through the use of reason, through the use of emotion, and through the image you present of yourself in your writing. The final chapter concerns style.

No book on how to write persuasively can in itself create a persuasive writer. You must have a basic knowledge of grammar and usage, and you must have the desire and the stamina to practice new skills. If you possess such qualifications, however, this book can help you to develop techniques of organizing and presenting your ideas effectively—techniques that writers have been using successfully for centuries.

CONTENTS

THE ART OF PERSUASION

CHAPTER **1 PROOF STRUCTURE**

The basic principle of structure in any kind of prose composition is clarity. If a reader cannot follow your line of argument—or worse, if you *have* no line of argument—then you have no hope of writing persuasively. A reader must understand what you want to convince him of before you have any chance of doing so. For this reason, the foundation of persuasive writing is *proof structure*. *Proof*, in this special context, means anything that supports, illustrates, or amplifies a stated subject.

The fundamental unit of proof structure is a paragraph with a *topic sentence* stating what is to be proved and additional sentences providing the proof. Similarly, a larger block of prose—an essay, article, report, speech, or book—may have a *thesis sentence*, stating the main point to be proved in the whole piece, and paragraphs providing the proof. A *proof essay* (thesis sentence and proof paragraphs) and a *proof paragraph* (topic sentence and supporting sentences) are therefore structurally identical.

Most good writers use proof structure. They may do so instinctively and unconsciously; they may disguise it, but the structure is there nevertheless. Mastering the subtleties of proof structure takes years of practice, but a conscious awareness of its rules makes the process easier.

PROOF PARAGRAPHS

The following two examples are models of proof

paragraph structure. In the first one, the topic sentence presents a generalization, and the rest of the paragraph proves it with a series of instances.

For as long as I can remember—and my memory for such things goes back into the 1920s—we have been hearing about something called a "sexual revolution." Students of the flapper era, who identified themselves with the "lost generation," dated the revolt from World War I. Undergraduates of the thirties believed that it began with the Depression, when many young people found marriage impossible and consequently looked for other sexual outlets. Those of the fifties thought the sexual revolution was an aftermath of World War II and began when returning veterans encountered patriotic coeds. Today's undergraduates firmly believe that the revolt started about 1960 when they were in junior high and that it somehow is related to both the threat of nuclear war and the invention of the pill.

—PAUL WOODRING, *The Higher Learning in America*

In the next example, the topic sentence presents a broad generalization about the nature of science; the rest of the paragraph proves the statement first with a general discussion and then with a specific example.

All science is the search for unity in hidden likenesses. The search may be on a grand scale, as in the modern theories which try to link the fields of gravitation and electromagnetism. But we do not need to be browbeaten by the scale of science. There are discoveries to be made by snatching a small likeness from the air too, if it is bold enough. In 1935 the Japanese physicist Hideki Yukawa wrote a paper which can still give heart to a young scientist. He took as his starting point the known fact that waves of light can sometimes behave as if they were separate pellets. From this he reasoned that the forces which hold the nucleus of an atom together might sometimes also be observed as if they were solid pellets. A schoolboy can see how thin Yukawa's analogy is, and his teacher would be severe with it. Yet Yukawa without a blush calculated the mass of the pellet he expected to see, and waited. He was right; his meson was found, and a range of other mesons, neither the existence nor the nature of which had been suspected before. The likeness had borne fruit.

—J. BRONOWSKI, *Science and Human Values*

The relationship of statement and proof in these two paragraphs requiries that one sentence be broader in scope than all the rest. In the Woodring paragraph, the several instances support the statement that we have heard about sexual revolutions for a long time. In the Bronowski paragraph the single example of the Japanese physicist is subordinate to the general statement about all science. Moreover, in each paragraph the proof itself is arranged according to some principle of order: chronological in the Woodring paragraph and general-to-specific (a general statement followed by a specific discussion and example) in the Bronowski paragraph. To write proof paragraphs, a knowledge of both *subordination* and *order* is necessary.

Subordination

As you write a proof paragraph, your central idea will sometimes become entangled in supporting ideas and details—or it may disappear altogether. You think you know what you want to say, but somehow what you have written does not say it. In the next paragraph, the subordination is confused.

Much stress is placed on the idea of youth these days in the United States. No other country seems to have emphasized it as much; perhaps it is primarily a twentieth-century phenomenon. Fast cars, rock music, and a free, innocent attitude towards sex are also indicative of the modern era. It is hard to imagine a Victorian dancing the twist or talking openly about contraceptives. There are many things wrong with our period, but prudery is not among them. In this respect, at least, the present is a healthy time in which to be alive.

The central point of this paragraph is not clear. Is the author trying to prove that ours is a youth-oriented society or that it is a healthy, innocent one? The paragraph drifts from one to the other. A better paragraph would subordinate one of these two ideas to the other. The healthy, innocent quality of our society could be presented as the main topic, and the emphasis on youth as one indication of it—or vice versa.

The next paragraph successfully deals with several related facts, all of which have been clearly subordinated to the topic sentence at the beginning.

In no other occupation but politics is it expected that a man will sacrifice honors, prestige and his chosen career on a single issue. Lawyers, businessmen, teachers, doctors, all face difficult personal decisions involving their integrity—but few, if any, face them in the glare of the spotlight as do those in public office. Few, if any, face the same dread finality of decision that confronts a Senator facing an important call of the roll. He may want more time for his decision—he may believe there is something to be said for both sides—he may feel that a slight amendment could remove all difficulties—but when that roll is called he cannot hide, he cannot equivocate, he cannot delay—and he senses that his constituency, like the Raven in Poe's poem, is perched there on his Senate desk, croaking "Nevermore" as he casts the vote that stakes his political future.

—JOHN F. KENNEDY, *Profiles in Courage*

How to decide which idea is the most important in a paragraph and which ones are subordinate to it depends not only on the paragraph itself but also on the argument of the whole piece. Specific techniques that are helpful in making such decisions will be discussed later in this chapter.

Order

After writing the topic sentence of a paragraph, you must present the rest in a logical order. The Woodring and Bronowski paragraphs quoted above illustrate the ordering devices of chronology and general-to-specific. Other possibilities are

SPECIFIC-TO-GENERAL (usually with the topic
sentence last)
SIZE (the largest house . . . the smallest)
QUALITY (the most beautiful . . . the ugliest)

QUANTITY (the greatest number . . . the fewest)

DISTANCE (the nearest . . . the farthest)

ENUMERATION (three reasons for . . .)

IMPORTANCE (the most influential . . . a less influential)

And so on.

Occasionally a paragraph, or even an entire essay, will be organized according to one of these ordering devices. Usually, however, a number of different ones are used together, as in the next paragraph.

From the days of the Goths and the Huns, the battered continent of Europe has been subjected to a good many invasions. The earlier barbarian efforts were often attended by pillage and rapine. In more recent years, however, the invasions have sometimes (not, alas, always) taken technically more peaceful forms. In the 18th century, Europe suffered the Grand Tour, a leisurely inspection conducted by infuriatingly supercilious Englishmen. In the 19th century, it endured the organized mass tour, a form of torture for tourist and touree alike to which Mark Twain left an eloquent memorial in *Innocents Abroad*. In the early 20th century, it had to confront the Lost Generation, which for a decade filled the cafés of Paris and the beaches of Majorca with cries of creative joy and agony. But since the Second World War, it has had to face up to a new and more ominous challenge: invasion by families. And notably by American families.

—ARTHUR M. SCHLESINGER, JR., *The Politics of Hope*

In this paragraph the first sentence indicates

that two orders are to be used simultaneously: *chronology* (from the days of the Goths and the Huns) and *enumeration* (a good many invasions). The next two sentences add a third order, *quality* (the barbarian invasions and the peaceful ones). The order of *time*, although chronologically arranged throughout, is divided into progressively shorter periods—first the barbarian period to the eighteenth century, then the eighteenth and nineteenth centuries individually, and finally the twentieth century in two parts. The peaceful invasions are divided into two types, according to *quantity*: those of individuals and those of groups.

No author ever fully charts such intricate ordering devices in advance, but a general awareness of them and the ways they can be combined is necessary if you are to present your thoughts clearly. The next paragraph lacks clarity precisely because its ordering devices are jumbled.

There are many causes of student unrest in our universities today. First, students are more aware of national events than they used to be and more inclined to have opinions about them. Even more important, the Vietnam war has politicized students and forced them to take stands on the issues. In addition, students are no longer prepared to sit passively by and let others regulate their lives. Finally, students have heard about campus unrest for years before they enter college, and they go off to school without ivy-covered illusions about what they will find there. Another important cause of student unrest is the lack of relevance of many of the academic programs students find themselves forced into. They will complain about such programs and try to do something about them.

This paragraph uses two ordering devices: *enumeration* of the causes and *importance* of the causes. Yet neither order is developed consistently. The third (but not the last) cause of student unrest is introduced by the word *finally*; the relative importance of the causes goes from bad to worse to not-so-bad. The sentence about the Vietnam war is not an "even more important" cause but simply an example of the first cause. Although the topic sentence of this paragraph is clear enough, inconsistencies in its ordering devices make the proof confusing.

This problem can be avoided by keeping the ordering devices consistent and by using clear *directional signals*—words or phrases that indicate the kinds of ordering devices used. In the student unrest paragraph, the directional signals of enumeration are *first, in addition, finally,* and *another*. The directional signals of importance are *even more important* and *another important*. A simple rearrangement of these causes and their directional signals will clarify this paragraph.

There are many causes of student unrest in our universities today. Students are more aware of national events than they used to be and more inclined to have opinions about them; the Vietnam war, for example, has politicized students and forced them to take sides on the issues. Students are critical not only of national policies but also of those of their individual universities. They have heard about campus unrest for years before they enter college, and they go off to school without ivy-covered illusions about what they will find there. When they find a lack of relevance in the academic programs they are forced into, they say so and try to do something about the problem. Students are no longer willing to sit passively by and let others regulate their lives for them.

In this version of the paragraph, the ordering device is general-to-specific—national issues, then local ones, in each case followed by an example. The strong directional signal *not only . . . but also* helps the reader follow the paragraph's argument easily. The final sentence in the revised version, out of place in the original, now sums up the students' attitudes towards both national and local problems.

VARIATIONS IN PROOF STRUCTURE

Topic Sentence Last

Although the basic structure of a proof paragraph is topic sentence followed by proof, the reverse is also common, especially if the topic itself is surprising, unbelievable, or shocking. By gradually preparing your reader for such a topic, you have a greater chance of persuading him to accept it.

Another reason for placing the topic sentence last is for dramatic emphasis.

Recall how absurd the teaching of one's own

literature once seemed to the best literary scholars, to cultivated people generally. Compare that confidence with the extraordinary effort and concern that we now put into the teaching of modern literature, American literature, contemporary literature, freshman composition, public speaking, remedial reading, elementary grammar. Put into the picture, too, the extraordinary number of people, extremely intelligent, highly competent, perfectly civil and humane, to whom great literature means absolutely nothing, who manage to get along without Shakespeare and Tolstoy. When Napoleon asked Pierre Laplace how God figured in his theory of the universe, the great astronomer replied that he had no need of that hypothesis. There are now many intelligent people, active in the professions and sciences, who have no need of imaginative literature.

—ALFRED KAZIN, "Literature as a Necessity of Life"

Topic Sentence Second

Another variation in paragraph structure is to place the topic sentence second and to make the first sentence a transitional one. In the next example, the first sentence serves both as a summary of the previous paragraph and as a preface to the topic sentence that follows it. The phrase *not merely* is the directional signal that tells the reader where the paragraph is going.

Language is not merely a matter of words and inflections. We should neglect a very essential element if we failed to take account of the many conventional features . . .

—ALBERT C. BAUGH, *A History of the English Language*

The next example differs from the last in that the topic sentence introduces a contradiction rather than an extension of the idea summarized in the first sentence.

Marvell was obviously following an accepted literary pattern when he wrote the stanza about mountains. But his lyric poetry as a whole disproves the charge that seventeenth-century poets felt little response to Nature. . . .

—MARJORIE HOPE NICOLSON,
Mountain Gloom and Mountain Glory

By placing the topic sentence second, the author has made the transition between two paragraphs perfectly clear.

Other Variations

Some paragraphs have topic sentences in the middle or slightly towards the beginning or end. Others build up to a topic sentence and place it first in the next paragraph. Some paragraphs have no topic sentences at all. But statement followed by proof is the order most commonly used, and the most useful; and it has the virtues of simplicity and directness.

PROOF ESSAYS

The principles of proof paragraph structure generally apply to proof essay structure as well. The thesis sentence of the essay corresponds to the topic sentence of the paragraph;

and like the individual sentences of the paragraph, the paragraphs of the essay serve as proof of the whole essay. The problems of subordination and order are similar. You must decide which of the several ideas in your essay is the most important, which others should be subordinate to it, and which ordering devices should be used to direct the flow of thought, both in the essay as a whole and in its individual parts.

Since the thesis sentence of the essay governs the direction of the entire piece, it must be constructed carefully. It may be argued that an essay involves so many complicated thoughts that no one sentence can be expected to summarize them all. But in most cases, and certainly in most brief essays, a failure to isolate the most important idea is usually an indication of sloppy thinking, not profundity. If you cannot state in a single sentence what, above all else, you want to prove, you have probably not untangled your thinking on the subject, and your essay will lack clarity.

The standard position of the thesis sentence in a proof essay is at the beginning.

One of the most furious controversies in contemporary education is being waged over a false issue. This is the issue of required curriculums versus elective curriculums, prescription or free choice in education. One group maintains not only that a liberal education in a democracy should contain certain required *studies* but that this requirement entails a curriculum of completely prescribed *courses* for all students. The second group maintains that since a basic moral principle of democracy is equality of concern for all persons to realize their best capacities, and since individual needs, interests, and talents vary considerably, therefore to prescribe knowledge of certain subject matters and facility in certain skills for all students is to run counter to the philosophy of democracy.

—SIDNEY HOOK, *Education for Modern Man*

The first sentence of this paragraph states that the thesis of Hook's discussion concerns the falseness of an issue; the second sentence (the topic sentence of the paragraph) states what the issue is. The details of the paragraph illustrate the topic sentence; and the paragraph itself, since it is directly concerned with the false issue, supports the thesis.

For a short essay the scope of the thesis should be appropriately limited. To help narrow the scope, two approaches are useful.

Fact, Definition, and Quality

In a discussion of general reasoning, Cicero suggests that when you have a broad thesis to discuss, you should ask yourself whether it concerns a problem of fact, of definition, or of quality. Suppose your essay deals with the conflict between parents and a school board: you ask yourself, first, is there in *fact* a conflict between parents and board? Perhaps both groups agree on basic aims but are simply unable to communicate with each other. If so, you may have a thesis. Second, is the problem one of *definition*? Who are "the parents"? Are they a representative group? Is the school board? The distinction may be worth an essay.

Third, what is the *quality* of a particular issue? Is it better for a town to pay good salaries to its teachers or to keep taxes at their present levels? Several theses might be carved out of this issue. By restricting a broad thesis, you will avoid writing a series of empty generalizations.

Dialectic Approach

The conjunctions *although* and *because* can be useful in narrowing a thesis. First, write down a general thesis sentence, no matter how simplistic it may sound—for example, "We must begin paying our teachers decent salaries." Then preface the statement with an argument against the thesis and add a clause supporting it. Thus the thesis may become "Although the town is financially strapped, we must begin paying our teachers decent salaries, because too many good teachers are being forced to find better-paying jobs elsewhere." At this point, other *although* and *because* clauses may be added to the original thesis, or either one of the subordinate clauses may itself be transformed into a new thesis and subjected to the same *although-because* process. This pro-and-con, dialectic approach can lead to a jungle of conflicting arguments, but eventually a specific one may emerge that seems more important or more interesting than the rest—one that is worth developing into an essay.

These two methods of limiting a thesis are useful only at the initial stages of writing an essay. After you have constructed your thesis sentence, you must then establish a list of ideas related to it and work out the problems of subordination and order. You may plan to prove your thesis by discussing several topics, only to discover, as you list them, that one of these subordinate ideas begins to usurp most of the space at your disposal. You will now have to decide either to abridge your discussion of this particular point or else change the original thesis to account for the new emphasis. You may plan to arrange your material according to an order of importance, only to discover that most of your topics are of equal value. You will then have to decide either to reorganize according to an order of (say) time or to use an order of simple enumeration. Decisions originally made about subordination and order will often have to be altered during the actual writing of the essay.

A good way to avoid some of this reshuffling and reevaluating is to make a *topic outline* before you begin writing. Suppose that you want to write an attack on the widespread use of bleached white flour in American breads. Your thesis might be

Man cannot live by bread alone—not the way they make it today.

The topics developing this thesis might then be

1. Nutritional value of white flour
   High heat of milling process
   Chemicals used
   Result has less food value than paper bag it comes in

Residue (fed to animals) has more food value than the flour

2. Why white flour was developed
   Faster milling process discovered
   Desire to prevent spoilage
   Increased saleability
   Ignorance of nutrition
3. Why it continues to be used
   Convenience: white flour keeps longer (nothing to spoil)
   "Enriched" fallacy: 24 nutriants removed, four put back
   Ignorance: consumers don't know basic principles of nutrition
4. Whole-grain bread flours should be used
   Better nutrition
   Better taste
   More variety: wheat, rye, soy, corn, etc.
   Could almost live on *these* breads alone

In this outline, the order moves from the inadequacies of bleached white flour—and the reasons for them—to the advantages of using whole-grain products.

In place of a topic outline, some writers prefer a *paragraph outline*. They organize their thoughts in paragraph units and jot down fairly full topic sentences together with some indication of their development.

THESIS: Man cannot live by bread alone—not the way they make it today.

TOPIC SENTENCE NO. 1: The principal ingredient of most American bread is bleached

white flour, which has almost no food
value. High heat of milling process.
Chemicals used. . . .

TOPIC SENTENCE NO. 2: White flour, which was
developed about a century ago, was the
accidental result of a new and faster
milling process. Desire to prevent spoilage. Increased saleability. . . .

TOPIC SENTENCE NO. 3: Why then does bread
made with white flour continue to be pro-
duced, advertised, sold, and consumed?
Convenience. . . .

And so on.

Both methods of outlining have the same
purpose: to save you time. Revising outlines is
is faster than revising written drafts.

Once an essay is written, you should be able
to follow the progression of its argument by iso-
lating the topic sentences. The next example
lists topic sentences from a chapter in William
H. Whyte's *The Organization Man*. The thesis
of the chapter is that during the first part of
the twentieth century, various changes in America placed a strain on the Protestant Ethic.

Here, in the words of banker Henry Clews as
he gave some fatherly advice to Yale students in
1908, is the Protestant Ethic in purest form. . . .

It was an exuberantly optimistic ethic. If every-
one could believe that seeking his self-interest automatically improves the lot of all, then the application
of hard work should eventually produce a heaven
on earth. . . .

Without this ethic capitalism would have been impossible. . . .

But the very industrial revolution which this highly serviceable ethic begot in time began to confound it. . . .

As organizations continued to expand, the Protestant Ethic bceame more and more divergent from the reality The Organization was itself creating. . . .

Thrift, for example. How can the organization man be thrifty? Other people are thrifty *for* him. He still buys most of his life insurance, but . . .

"Hard work?" . . .

Self-reliance? . . .

I have been talking of the impact of organization on the Protestant Ethic; just as important, however, was the intellectual assault. . . .

It is not in the province of this book to go into a diagnosis of the ideas of Dewey and James and the other pragmatists. But . . .

Critics of pragmatism, and followers too, should remember the context of the times in which the pragmatists made their case. . . .

Pragmatism's emphasis on the social and the practical, furthermore, was thoroughly in the American tradition. . . .

Reform was everywhere in the air. By the time of the First World War . . .

The ground, in short, was ready, and . . .

—WILLIAM H. WHYTE, JR., *The Organization Man*

Although a few topic sentences merely expanding or qualifying a point have been omitted from this example, the ones given here clearly reveal Whyte's structure. First, he shows how the Protestant Ethic nourished capitalism. Then he shows how the organizational aspect of capitalism and the philosophy of pragmatism together helped to undermine the Protestant

Ethic. In your own essays a similar check of topic sentences should reveal the progression of your argument.

To write clearly requires both a knowledge of proof structure and a great deal of practice. In writing an essay and the individual paragraphs within it, always ask yourself: *What am I trying to prove?* Do not be discouraged at the number of drafts and false starts you may have to discard. An essay that seems to be clearly and effortlessly written is generally the product of many drafts.

BEGINNINGS AND ENDINGS CHAPTER 2

BEGINNINGS

An essay can always begin with the thesis sentence, continue to the end of the last paragraph, and stop. But beginning with the thesis sentence is often too abrupt, and other techniques may be preferable. The most common of these usually employ one or more of the following elements: (1) an *exordium*, arousing sympathy and interest; (2) a *narrative*, giving the general background of the subject; and (3) a *partition*, stating the thesis and, possibly, the way it will be developed. All three of these elements are apparent in the next example.

The great tragic artists of the world are four, and three of them are Greek. It is in tragedy that the pre-eminence of the Greeks can be seen most clearly. Except for Shakespeare, the great three, Aeschylus, Sophocles, Euripides, stand alone. Tragedy is an achievement peculiarly Greek. They were the first to perceive it and they lifted it to its supreme height. Nor is it a matter that directly touches only the great artists who wrote tragedies; it concerns the entire people as well, who felt the appeal of the tragic to such a degree that they would gather thirty thousand strong to see a performance. In tragedy the Greek genius penetrated farthest and it is the revelation of what was most profound in them.

—EDITH HAMILTON, *The Greek Way*

The reader's interest is caught by the assertive first sentence of this paragraph (exordium).

The author then amplifies the opening statement and gives the general background of the subject (narrative). The last sentence presents (in the order in which they will be developed) the two parts of the thesis (partition). Although the three elements may be isolated for the purpose of identification, they are joined together smoothly in this paragraph.

Often one or two of these elements are partially merged in an opening section. A narrative, for example, may be presented in such a striking manner that the requirements of the exordium are also satisfied. In the following paragraphs, several common techniques of combining these elements are illustrated.

Definition

In the guise of defining a term, the background of an issue is presented (narrative), and the need to discuss it becomes apparent (exordium). The thesis (partition) is announced in the second paragraph.

In a very real sense, Harlem is the capital of Black America. And America has always been divided into black and white, and the substance of the division is social, economic, and cultural. But even the name Harlem, now, means simply Negroes (even though some other peoples live there too). The identification is international as well: even in Belize, the capital of predominantly Negro British Honduras, there are vendors who decorate their carts with flowers and the names or pictures of Negro culture heroes associated with Harlem like

Sugar Ray Robinson. Some of the vendors even wear t-shirts that say "Harlem, U.S.A.," and they speak about it as a black Paris. In Havana a young Afro-Cuban begged me to tell him about the "big leg ladies" of Lenox Avenue, hoping, too, that I could provide some way for him to get to that mystic and romantic place.

There are, I suppose, contained within the central mythology of Harlem, almost as many versions of its glamour, and its despair, as there are places with people to make them up. . . .

—LE ROI JONES, *Home*

This technique is useful when your thesis has a term that needs defining or one (in this case *Harlem*) that is used in a special sense.

Personal History

The author draws attention to himself. By describing his own unique or gilt-edged credentials (exordium), he introduces the background of his subject (narrative), and then his thesis (partition).

Some 13 years ago, a book of mine was published by the name of *Cybernetics*. In it I discussed the problems of control and communication in the living organism and the machine. I made a considerable number of predictions about the development of controlled machines and about the corresponding techniques of automatization, which I foresaw as having important consequences affecting the society of the future. Now, 13 years later, it seems appropriate to take stock of the present position with respect to both cybernetic technique and the social consequences of this technique.

—NORBERT WIENER, "Some Moral and Technical Consequences of Automation"

In using this technique, be sure that the reference to yourself is not egotistical.

Discovery

The reader's interest is aroused (exordium) by announcing a new and valuable insight into a subject that has been generally misunderstood. The background of the subject (narrative) emerges as the author demonstrates how great the misconception is. The thesis (partition) appears at the end of the paragraph.

Anyone who has been fortunate enough to eat fresh home-cooked vegetables in France remembers them with pleasure, with trembling nostalgia: "Those delicious little green beans! They even serve them as a separate course!" There are those who are convinced that it is only in France that one can enjoy such experiences because French vegetables are somehow different. Fortunately this is not the case. Any fine, fresh vegetable in season will taste just as good in America or anywhere else when you use the French vegetable-cooking techniques.

—JULIA CHILD, *The French Chef Cookbook*

These three techniques—definition, personal history, and discovery—are plain, clear, and businesslike. You can also use the following more lively ones, in which the attention-getting purpose of the exordium obscures or even eliminates the narrative and the partition.

The Anecdote

If it draws attention to the central thesis, an anecdote can be effective, but it must be brief in comparison with the bulk of the essay.

"Hell, I hire anybody," Harold Ross told Ralph Ingersoll in the summer of 1925 when Ingersoll called on the editor of the *New Yorker*, asked for a job, and got one. It wasn't as simple as it sounds, though. Ingersoll had appeared in the editor's office dressed in a Palm Beach suit he had bought for the occasion, and Ross had talked to him for only a few minutes, gesticulating widely, when his big right hand struck an inkwell. Suddenly Ingersoll's new suit was dripping with ink and Ross was covered with embarrassment. Ingersoll had almost reached the office door on what he was sure was his way out of Ross's life when the editor shouted, "You're hired!" And then, a few moments later, sighed, "Hell, I hire anybody."

From then on Ross hired anybody, and everybody, in his frantic and ceaseless search for the Fountain of Perfection. . . .

—JAMES THURBER, *The Years With Ross*

Mystery

This attention-getting technique introduces an incident or problem that the following discussion is designed to resolve.

When I was young in the Midwest and had

dreams of my own, it seemed to me a fine thing to live as the Fitzgeralds had, where every gesture had a special flair that marked it as one's own. Together they personified the immense lure of the East, of young fame, of dissolution and early death —their sepia-tinted photographs in rotogravure sections across the country: Scott, in an immaculate Norfolk jacket, gesturing nervously with a cigarette, Zelda brightly at his side, her clean wild hair brushed back from her face. But it was not her beauty that was arresting. It was her style, a sort of insolence toward life, her total lack of caution, her fearless and abundant pride. If the Fitzgeralds were ghostly figures out of an era that was gone, they had nevertheless made an impact on the American imagination that reverberated into my own generation. I wanted to know why.

—NANCY MILFORD, *Zelda*

The danger in using this technique is the temptation to be overly dramatic. Do not use it unless your material does in fact have an element of mystery about it.

The Pertinent Quotation

As the year 1966 was drawing to a close, Professor Charles Susskind of the University of California summed up his opinions of the student demonstrators on the Berkeley campus in these words: "I don't know why they think of themselves as the New Left. Their methods look to me much more like those of the Nazi students whom I saw in the 1930s harassing deans, hounding professors and their families, making public disturbances, and interfering with lectures, until only professors sympathetic to the Nazi cause remained."

The professor's comparison of the New Left with the Old Right is not only apt but just.

—MAX GELTMAN, "The New Left and The Old Right"

The Bon Mot

Madison Avenue also, I imagine, is paved with good intentions. It would be strange if it weren't, what with exhibiting so many other likenesses to Hell. . . .

—LOUIS KRONENBERGER, The Cart and the Horse

The Literary Allusion

This is a rather presumptuous title ["Getting at Truth"] for a biographer to use, since truth is a very large word. In the sense that it means the reality about a human being it is probably impossible for a biographer to achieve. In the sense that it means a reasonable presentation of all available facts it is more nearly possible, but even this limited goal is harder to reach than it appears to be. A biographer needs to be both humble and cautious when he remembers the nature of the material he is working with, for a historical fact is rather like the flamingo that Alice in Wonderland tried to use as a croquet mallet. As soon as she got its neck nicely straightened out and was ready to hit the ball, it would turn and look at her with a puzzled expression, and any biographer knows that what is called a "fact" has a way of doing the same.

—MARCHETTE CHUTE, "Getting at Truth"

The ways of beginning an essay described and illustrated above are effective only if they are presented with restraint and taste. The beginning section should never outweigh the rest of the paper; nor should it draw undue attention to itself. Avoid the following:

The Overly Dramatic Approach
> The sound of shots and the shriek of sirens broke the still night air. . . .

The Shirtsleeves Approach
> Here I am at the old typewriter trying for the third time to write a paper on . . .

The Chummy Approach
> Well, I bet you never stopped to think that . . .

The Artistic Approach
> Thump. Thump. Thump. Three knocks at the door. I knew it could only be . . .

The High-Altitude Approach
> Since the beginning of recorded time, mankind has always tried . . .

The Apologetic Approach
> Of course it's just my opinion, but for what it's worth, I think that . . .

The Overly Mechanical Approach
> The purpose of this essay is to discuss . . .

Although the techniques of definition, personal history, discovery, anecdote, mystery, pertinent quotation, bon mot, and literary allusion described in this section can all be used effectively, do not forget the plain straightforward technique of thesis sentence followed by topic sentence number one; it is often your best and clearest opening.

> The aims, methods, and organization of the American college are open to such serious question that the college itself may not be long for this world.
> Its condition is obscured by its reputation. A college degree is now regarded as the passport to "success." We are told . . .
>
> —ROBERT M. HUTCHINS, "Colleges Are Obsolete"

ENDINGS

The ending of an essay should be brief, and it should draw attention to the central part of your thesis. It should never be glued to the body of your paper with a deadly, mechanical phrase such as *in conclusion, thus we have seen,* or *thus it is clear.* For a long essay (but almost never for a short one) a straightforward summary of major points is often effective. If your essay builds to a conclusion, its ending may be the thesis sentence itself. Otherwise, one of the following techniques may be used.

The Frame

This technique prepares for the ending of the essay in the beginning. You might start, for example, with a striking quotation or anecdote which is recalled at the end: the body of the paper is thus "framed." The next example is the final section of the Marchette Chute essay whose beginning (see page 28) refers to the croquet game in *Alice in Wonderland.*

The reason Alice had so much trouble with her flamingo is that the average flamingo does not wish to be used as a croquet mallet. It has other purposes in view. The same thing is true of a fact, which can be just as self-willed as a flamingo and has its own kind of stubborn integrity. To try to force a series of facts into a previously desired arrangement is a form of misuse to which no self-respecting fact will willingly submit itself. The best and only way to treat it is to leave it alone and be willing to follow where it leads, rather than to press your own wishes upon it.

To put the whole thing into a single sentence: you will never succeed in getting at the truth if you think you know, ahead of time, what the truth ought to be.

—MARCHETTE CHUTE, "Getting at Truth"

Occasionally the ending picks up material introduced in the middle rather than in the beginning of an essay, but the principle is the same.

The Shift-of-Level

An essay in this form concludes with a relatively short section that shifts to a different level of the same discussion and then stops. For example, the body of the essay might examine the elements of a typical Broadway musical, and then the conclusion might refer to the development of that art form in the rock musical *Hair*. Or the body of the essay might describe the need for high-speed transportation between cities, and then the conclusion might refer to a similar need (or lack of need) for high-speed transportation between continents.

The shift-of-level ending is used for the essay concerning the plight of the American college (see page 30). After analyzing the various problems of colleges as they now exist, the author concludes his essay by suggesting a remedy.

Suppose we took the four years beginning with the junior year in high school and ending with the sophomore year in college and created an institution dedicated to liberal education. The teachers assembled should be . . .

―ROBERT M. HUTCHINS, "Colleges are Obsolete"

Although the frame and shift-of-level techniques are neat and professional, the best ending is often the shortest. You may therefore want simply to give the last sentence of your essay an air of finality, and leave it at that.

CHAPTER 3
THE APPEAL
TO REASON

The first two chapters of this book are concerned with the structure of an essay; the next three are concerned with traditional techniques of persuasion: the appeal to reason, the appeal to emotion, and the ethical appeal (the appeal derived from the character of the author).

The appeal to reason rests on the psychological fact that the reader likes to think of himself as a rational being. He will probably be swayed by his emotions and by his opinion of you as an author; but he likes to think, at best, that he is being reasonable in assessing your arguments. The object is to present your case in such a way that you appeal to his sense of reasonableness.

THE GENERAL PROBLEM
OF APPEALING TO REASON

There are two kinds of logic used in all arguments. The first is *inductive*—the process of gathering and judging specific evidence to arrive at a general conclusion. To prove that war is destructive, you cite the specific examples of London, Dresden, and Hiroshima. The other kind of logic is *deductive*—the process of deriving a specific conclusion from general premises, as in the famous syllogism: All men are mortal beings / Socrates is a man / Therefore, Socrates is a mortal being. Both kinds of logic are subject to fallacies. To help you avoid them in your own writing or to discover them in that of an opponent, seven of the most common fallacies of logic are listed below.

Oversimplification

The presentation of an either-or alternative. You argue that one can either be for women's liberation or against it.

Equivocation

A shift in the meaning of a term. At the beginning of your discussion, the word *democracy* means "participatory government"; later, it assumes the meaning of "representative government."

Circular Argument

Assuming what is to be proved. You argue that it is inhumane to build a shopping center in a ghetto, because evictions are so cruel. (*I.e.*, it is inhumane because it is inhumane.)

Red Herring

The introduction of a false issue to draw attention away from the real one. In apologizing for the President's failure to keep a certain campaign promise, you argue that politicians rarely do keep such promises.

Begging the Question

Assuming a conclusion that has not been established. Instead of showing why a certain plan is unworkable, you argue that the "unworkable plan" should be replaced by another.

Complex Question

Asking a questoin in such a way that it conceals an unjustified assumption. You ask why the Mayor won't consider a compromise. (Won't he?)

Ad Populum ("to the people")

Avoiding a specific issue by appealing to a popular prejudice. You argue that the proposal to withdraw from a war without total victory is un-American.

Any argument may be subject to such fallacies in logic; it may also be challenged at its very foundation. Inductive logic may be questioned on the ground of insufficient evidence: because you have never seen a purple cow does not *prove* that one does not exist somewhere. Similarly, the general premise of any deductive argument may be questioned: perhaps all men are *not* mortal beings. In short, any argument, no matter how basic, implies the possibility of a counter-argument, and thus arises the need of *refutation*—the process of defending an argument (1) by undercutting possible objections to it or (2) by attacking established alternatives to it.

Refutation may be confined to a specific section of an essay, or blended into the general discussion—or both. The alternative you choose in a particular case depends on the relative strength either of your own argument or of that of your opposition. If there is a particularly strong alternative argument, you may want to include a wholly separate section of refutation, placed either at the beginning of your essay (thereby establishing the need for your own corrective argument), or just before a strong, reaffirming conclusion. In most cases, however, it is better simply to refute objections to your own argument as they come up.

If you are faced with the problem of using insufficient evidence, your best defense is to admit the problem openly. By demonstrating your own uneasiness in accepting the evidence, you encourage your reader to trust your judgment.

Statistical workers gathered what figures they could on the effects of the bomb. They reported that 78,150 people had been killed, 13,983 were missing, and 37,425 had been injured. No one in the ctiy government pretended that these figures were accurate—though the Americans accepted them as official—and as the months went by and more and more hundreds of corpses were dug up from the ruins, and as the number of unclaimed urns of ashes at the Zempoji Temple in Koi rose into the thousands, the statisticians began to say that at least a hundred thousand people had lost their lives in the bombing. . . .

—JOHN HERSEY, *Hiroshima*

Similarly, in presenting your conclusions, protect yourself from criticism by openly acknowledging any possible weaknesses.

This is my interpretation; it cannot be proved.

While it is based on a long study of the facts, it is nevertheless subjective, and has no standing as history. For me this interpretation fits into the pattern of Johnson's life as it has been built up in my mind. Moreover, . . .

—JAMES L. CLIFFORD, "A Biographer Looks at Dr. Johnson"

Or tell the reader that you do not exaggerate or oversimplify your conclusions.

I do not want to exaggerate. This kind of writing is not yet universal, and . . .

—GEORGE ORWELL, "Politics and the English Language"

In being critical about the quality of your evidence and about the process of deriving a conclusion from it, you have helped to refute possible objections to your arguments; and by demonstrating an attitude of objectivity, you have appealed to the reasonableness of your reader.

KINDS OF ARGUMENT

Many kinds of argument may be used in support of almost any thesis. The discussion that follows deals with several of the more common ones, and with some special problems of their refutation.

The Nature of a Thing

Everything from a tree to a bassoon, from a mathematical theorem to the smell of roses, can be said to have its nature—its ideal or universal state of being, its bassoon-ness or its smell-of-roses-ness. If something contradicts that state of being (a bassoon with leaves, a theorem that smells of roses), its nature is contradicted. Conversely, if something is in keeping with its universal state of being, it is in keeping with its nature. Socrates is a mortal being because it is the nature of man to die. A given plant is a tree because it possesses all the qualities associated with the universal state of tree-ness.

To argue from the nature of a thing may involve generally accepted assumptions (all men are mortal beings); it may also involve a definition of what you yourself think a universal state of being should include. Suppose you want to argue that a particular university should adopt a policy of open enrollment. You could use other kinds of argument to support your case, such as testimony (a respected figure who agrees with you) or history (the trend in modern education towards equal opportunity); but an argument from the nature of a thing would require a definition of what you think the ideal of a university includes. You might argue that a university is an integral part of the community and that any attempt by one group (the administration) to exclude another (certain students) contradicts that concept. Such an assertion is clearly open to debate, and it requiries considerable support.

The technique of arguing from the nature of a thing is shown in the next example.

What's transportation for? This is a question

that highway engineers apparently never ask themselves: probably because they take for granted the belief that transportation exists for the purpose of providing suitable outlets for the motorcar industry. To increase the number of cars, to enable motorists to go longer distances, to more places, at higher speeds, has become an end in itself. Does this overemployment of the motorcar not consume ever larger quantities of gas, oil, concrete, rubber, and steel, and so provide the very groundwork for an expanding economy? Certainly, but none of these make up the essential purpose of transportation. The purpose of transportation is to bring people or goods to places where they are needed, and to concentrate the greatest variety of goods and people within a limited area, in order to widen the possibility of choice without making it necessary to travel. A good transportation system minimizes unnecessary transportation; and in any event, it offers a change of speed and mode to fit a diversity of human purposes.

—LEWIS MUMFORD, *The Highway and the City*

Since any argument based on the nature of a thing depends heavily on assertion, it may be challenged by a strong counter-argument— the claim that the author has not truly seen the real nature of the thing under discussion. You could argue here, for example, that the purpose of transportation is not only to bring people to places where they are *needed*, but also to provide them a means for going where they *want* to go. In order to protect an argument based on the nature of a thing from such a challenge, therefore, you must present the strongest possible supporting evidence. A reader should immediately be struck with the basic soundness of your definition.

Authority

Standard authorities, such as the *Encyclopedia Britannica*, the *Oxford English Dictionary*, and even individuals whose prestige is long-established (Aristotle, Darwin) may help to support a thesis, but not if they are introduced with uncritical acceptance. For example, an uncritical reference to *Webster* ("Webster says that . . .") would only demonstrate your ignorance of the *many* dictionaries using that name in their titles. If you use a standard authority, therefore, be respectful but not subservient.

> There are, as Aristotle has pointed out, two main ways in which a man's power of reflection becomes active. They are called, in Aristotle's language, *theoretikos* and *praktikos* respectively; which is to say, thinking about what is actually the case and thinking about what had better be done. In English translation the words *contemplative* and *operative* probably come closest to Aristotle's intent. To think contemplatively is to ask oneself what *is*; to think operatively is to ask oneself what to *do*.
>
> —PHILIP WHEELWRIGHT, *A Critical Introduction to Ethics*

Wheelwright does not claim that the distinction between contemplative and operative thinking is valid *because* Aristotle says so; he simply agrees with Aristotle.

Personal testimony is another form of authority; but like standard authorities, it should never be offered uncritically. The person you cite should preferably be unbiased and, in fact, an authority.

The psychotherapist Dr. Otto Rank once

remarked in his latter years of practice that practically all the women who came to him had problems because their husbands were not assertive enough. Despite the oversimplified sound of this sentence, it contains a telling point: our effete cultivation of sex can make us so intellectual and detached about it that the simple power of the act evaporates, and we lose—and this loss is especially serious for women—the important elemental pleasure of "being taken," being "carried away." . . .

—ROLLO MAY, "Antidotes for the New Puritanism"

Personal testimony is always most effective when used together with detailed, factual evidence.

Cause and Effect

This argument analyzes a present condition based on a previous cause, or it predicts a future condition based on a present cause. In the next paragraph, philanthropy is cited as the immediate cause for the excellence of American observatories and medical research institutions.

Science did not begin to receive the encouragement of significant patronage in this country until the turn of the century. It was then that the first giant fortunes accumulated in the American industrial revolution became available for such nonutilitarian enterprises as the advancement of learning. In testimony to the patrons' aspiration to dissociate their philanthropy from the harsh world of industry and commerce, the largest sums went to astronomy and medical research. Consequently, it was in these fields that American science first established claim to world eminence. No other nation's scientific establishment approaches the American in the magnificence of its observatories, and the United States excels all other nations in the number of first-rate medical research institutions per unit of population.

—GERARD PIEL, *Science in the Cause of Man*

This technique of argument can fail to be persuasive if a cause does not seem adequate in itself to produce the effect or if it does not seem to be the most probable. You could argue here, for example, that it takes much more than money to produce scientific progress or that a general stress on scientific education since the two world wars is a more important cause of this progress than philanthropy. In using the technique of cause and effect yourself, therefore, you may want to include certain qualifications. You can, for example, admit that yours is not the only possible cause or even the major one.

I am not suggesting that Carlyle was the decisive influence on Marx in this respect, though his was certainly an important influence. . . .

—RAYMOND WILLIAMS, "Prelude to Alienation"

Another effective method of defense is to discuss the objections to your case and then to reassert or revise your own position.

Weber's analysis of the importance of the Calvinist idea of a "calling" to the rise of capitalism has been widely disputed. Some economic historians like Henri Pirenne have claimed to trace the capitalist spirit well back into the Middle Ages before the Reformation (and Marx once admitted in a letter to being puzzled as to why capitalism had not developed in Rome at the time of Christ, all of its preconditions having been fulfilled). Yet whatever the specific weight of the Protestant ethic in *determining* the rise of capitalism, there is little doubt that its distinctive spirit was part of the event. If Puritanism was not the godfather to capitalism, then it was godson. As cause or effect, the ethical and religious importance of hard work became a constituent principle of the capitalist West.

—MICHAEL HARRINGTON, *The Accidental Century*

Comparisons

Comparisons can help to present a point clearly and in depth.

The separate-but-equal doctrine was promulgated by the Supreme Court in 1896. It had the same purpose domestically as the Open Door Policy toward China in the international arena: to stabilize a situation and subordinate a non-white population so that racist exploiters could manipulate those people according to their own selfish interests. . . .

—ELDRIDGE CLEAVER, *Soul on Ice*

The technique of comparison may be challenged by pointing out exceptions or alternatives or by showing that the comparison itself is irrelevant. You could argue here, for example, that American race relations and a Chinese commercial treaty in fact have little to do with each other, that the former was emotional in origin and the latter coldly imperialistic. When you use the technique of comparison yourself, therefore, you may need to include certain qualifications before reasserting your basic argument.

This, of course, is comparing a French "ideal" type of introduction to sex with an American "ideal" type. In actuality, there are as many variations in France as in the United States in the ways youth is introduced to sex. Still . . .

—BRUNO BETTELHEIM, "Youth: Change and Challenge"

Or stress differences in order to affirm similarities.

Not all large organizations are alike, despite the sorts of institutional similarities investigated by sociologists, and, of course, not all positions in them are alike. Many, although their top executives clamor for creativity and independence of mind, largely manage to process these qualities out of "their" people in the lower ranks. Others stockpile talent and expect it to keep as gold keeps at Fort Knox. Still others make products or provide services which are either antisocial or useless. But here and there one finds companies which face real and not contrived problems and apply to them an intelligence which is often remarkably disinterested and, in the best sense of the word, "academic." Young people in search of challenge and development would do well to seek out such relatively productive climates, rather than to assume offhand that these (as is true of so many brand-name products) are all alike except for the advertising and the label.

—DAVID REISMAN, "Where Is the College Generation Headed?"

Figurative comparisons such as similes and metaphors can sometimes be effective in swaying a reader's attitude, especially if they are not labored or used too frequently. They differ from straight comparisons in that the objects compared are different in kind. A *simile* uses the word *like* or *as* in its comparison (red as a rose); a *metaphor* omits these words and describes one object in terms of another (love is a bed of roses).

Much of the persuasive value of similes and metaphors—and also of straight comparisons—depends on the connotations they arouse. The next example uses a metaphor with connotations of grandeur (a mighty tree) to support the conservative view that changes in society should evolve slowly.

> Society is a living organism with roots deep in the past. The true community, the Conservative likes to say, is a tree, not a machine. It rose to its present strength and glory through centuries of growth, and men must forbear to think of it as a mechanical contrivance that can be dismantled and reassembled in one generation. Not fiat but prescription, not the open hand of experiment but the hidden hand of custom, is the chief creative force in the social process.
>
> —CLINTON ROSSITER, *Conservatism in America*

Although similes and metaphors can be effective, they should be used sparingly and never in place of solid evidence. Without additional support, Rossiter's argument can easily be refuted: the true community is *in fact* neither a tree nor a machine.

An *analogy* is a special kind of comparison. It usually involves an explanation or illustration of one thing in terms of another that is markedly different in most respects. Again, the connotations aroused by the comparison add greatly to the persuasive power of the argument. In the next example, the threat of environmental pollution is compared with the threat of a military invasion.

When an enemy tries to overrun the country, we seem to be able to get together and set narrow privileges aside for a little while until victory has been won. Why not do the same in fighting the enemy within our midst? And don't forget that the forces which tend to destroy our natural resources are many, and with the rapidly growing population they will be even stronger in the future. It is up to those who recognize the value of these resources to band together in programs which will spread the word—that conservation of all our resources is essential to preserve our way of living.

—ARIE J. HAAGEN-SMIT, "The Troubled Outdoors"

Historical analogies are closely related to cause and effect. They help to create an objective view of topical problems and to influence a reader's reaction, particularly if the issue is volatile or emotionally charged. A reference to history can give the impression that you yourself are cool and reasonable and that what you have to say rests on a sound knowledge of the past. The next paragraph is taken from a discussion of student uprisings.

Our present crisis is not the worst we have had. Actually, the stormiest era in the history of American colleges was from about 1880 to 1895, when strikes, demonstrations, violence and resignations erupted at Dartmouth, Union, Bowdoin, Wesleyan, Amherst, Middlebury. In 1883, for instance, "the greatest rebellion in Bowdoin's history" saw the outbreak of several riots against its military president, Maj. Gen. Joshua Chamberlain. Eleven sophomores had been expelled for involvement in a hazing incident; thereupon almost the entire studentry went on strike, and the General resigned. At Union College in 1888, the entire student body demonstrated behind a drum corps in Schenectady's main street; undaunted by a snowstorm, they demanded the appointment of a new president. They had their own candidate, a professor who had led them in their fight against the previous incumbent, and they got their man. Students and professors in this era held public "trials" of their presidents; Dartmouth and Hamilton were among those which saw such proceedings.

—LEWIS S. FEUER, "Should College Students Grade Their Teachers?"

These references to student uprisings nearly a century ago help one to view any recent crisis with more objectivity; and the knowledge that Bowdoin and Union somehow did survive adds weight to any solution one might want to support for a Berkeley, a Columbia, or a Kent State.

The use of historical analogies introduces special problems, however. First, there is a widespread assumption that history repeats itself. Whatever the truth of this assumption, it can be dangerous to make too close a connection between past and present (a Bowdoin or Union of a century ago is *not* a modern Berkeley or Columbia). Second, there is the danger of the *post hoc, ergo propter hoc* (*after* this and therefore *because* of this) fallacy, which assumes that because Y occurred after X, then X is *necessarily* the cause of Y: that, for example, because a road was full of potholes, the automobile accident occurred. (The accident may not have been caused by the potholes.) When you use an historical analogy, therefore, discuss its weaknesses openly and strengthen it as much as possible. In the next paragraph, Barbara Ward defends her analogy between the indifference of the eighteenth-century French aristocracy to the peasants and the indifference of wealthy nations to poor ones today.

The analogy is not irrelevant. What nations do is determined by what nations think and many of the attitudes that paralyzed effective action before earlier catastrophes can be discerned in Western public opinion today. The Marie Antoinette class in our Western society are the indifferent who, absorbed in the new expanding wealth of the mass consumption economy, simply do not see the misery piling up beyond the charmed frontiers of their Atlantic citadel. The fact that at least half the citizens in the Atlantic world now enjoy better health, food, and comfort than the aristocrats of two centuries ago only makes the spread of indifferent affluence more all-embracing and deprives radical protest of much of its local pressure.

> —BARBARA WARD, "Hindsight and Foresight in the World Economy"

Proverbs, Aphorisms, and Literary References

Proverbs and aphorisms are short, pithy statements of principle, precept, or fundamental truth. *Proverb* implies an oral tradition expressed in a plain or blunt style; *aphorism* implies specific authorship and stylistic elegance. The traditional (but by no means only) source of proverbs is the Bible. Well-known sources of aphorisms include the fables of Aesop and Benjamin Franklin's *Poor Richard's Almanack*.

Although proverbs and aphorisms have the ring of truth, they should be used with restraint. Remember that each one can usually be answered with another that is equally effective; for a "He who hesitates is lost" there is a "Look before you leap." Use these devices to reinforce your argument, but not to establish it. There is no substitute for solid, factual evidence.

Literary references have the same strengths and weaknesses as proverbs and aphorisms, and they are best used to confirm rather than to establish arguments.

Personal relations are despised today. They are regarded as bourgeois luxuries, as products of a time of fair weather which is now past, and we are urged to get rid of them, and to dedicate ourselves to some movement or cause instead. I hate the idea of causes, and if I had to choose between betraying my country and betraying my friend, I hope I should have the guts to betray my country. Such a choice may scandalize the modern reader, and he may stretch out his patriotic hand to the telephone at once and ring up the police. It would not have shocked Dante, though. Dante places Brutus and Cassius in the lowest circle of Hell because they had chosen to betray their friend Julius Caesar rather than their country Rome. Probably one will not be asked to make such an agonizing choice. Still . . .

—E. M. FORSTER, "What I Believe"

A literary reference is most effective when its source (in this case the *Divine Comedy*) is

recognized by the reader, but the meaning of
the paragraph must never depend upon this
recognition.

THE USE OF ARGUMENT

Specific kinds of persuasive arguments are
rarely used in isolation. In a single paragraph,
several are often employed, as in the next
example, which concerns the merging of ethnic
characteristics in America.

No stock, once it has come to America, remains
what it was. Each breeds away from type, both by
the influence of the new physical environment and
by the fact of intermingling. Every stock, by its
migration, breaks with its past environment and
enters a new one. Continued migration from one
American region to another and mobility from one
class and therefore one set of living standards to
another continue the process of environmental
reconditioning. How substantial the changes may
be was shown in 1912 in the classic study by Franz
Boas, *Changes in Bodily Form of Descendants of
Immigrants.* Despite the prevailing view that skull
measurements are an unchanging racial charac-
teristic, Boas showed that the skull indices of the
children of Jewish and Italian immigrants differed
appreciably from those of the parents. This is
environmental change away from ethnic type,
whether due to diet, living standards, climate, or
other factors in the natural and cultural environment. Boas was dealing with the physical factor
that one would expect to be most resistant to
change. What applied to skull changes would apply
more easily to psychic and cultural changes; and

what applied under the influence of environmental and standard-of-living change would apply more easily as the result of biological mixture.

—MAX LERNER, *America as a Civilization*

The topic of the paragraph, that no ethnic stock remains unchanged in America, is supported by the arguments of *cause and effect* (the change is caused by the new physical environment and by intermingling); *the nature of a thing* (migration is a change of environment); *cause and effect* (continued migration and class mobility cause environmental reconditioning); *standard authority* (Boas); *the nature of a thing* (the difference in skull indices is ethnic change, no matter what its cause); *comparison* (physical changes as opposed to psychic and cultural changes); and a *comparison* of *cause and effect* (the influence of environmental and standard-of-living change as opposed to the result of biological mixture). Such a combination of argumentative techniques may seem complex, but it is more typical of usual practice than many of the other examples given in this chapter.

Knowing various kinds of argument is particularly useful when you are looking for ways to prove a thesis. Suppose, for example, that you wish to prove that the United States should solve some of its domestic problems before throwing any more money into the space race. Each kind of argument described in this chapter can suggest a way to support your thesis.

The Nature of a Thing

The first priority of government is to lessen

the needs of the governed; as long as slums exist in the United States, there can be no justification for spending a penny on the space race.

Cause and Effect
The enormous amount of money put into the program reduces the amount available for urban renewal and mass transit.

Personal Testimony
A quotation from Joseph Wood Krutch's celebrated essay, "Why I am Not Going to the Moon."

Literary Reference
Let *the cow* jump over the moon.

And so on.

You will not want to *organize* your essay according to the different kinds of argument, but mentally running over the list can help you *find* something to say about practically anything.

CHAPTER 4 THE APPEAL TO EMOTION

Every written argument, no matter how factual and objective, has some kind of emotional impact on a reader and reveals some image of its author. Even if you want to, you cannot avoid using the appeal to emotion and the appeal based on your character as an author (the ethical appeal). Although these appeals, because they are not immediately apparent, may seem underhanded or even sinister, an ignorance of how they work can arouse an undesired emotional response or produce a wrong image of yourself as a person. For these reasons, it is important to understand exactly how they both work. In Chapter 5, the ethical appeal is analyzed; this chapter concentrates on three aspects of the emotional appeal.

USE OF SPECIFIC DETAILS

If a discussion is vague and general, the emotional response of a reader will be one of boredom—if, indeed, his attention is engaged at all. Instead of talking about a subject, therefore, present the subject itself through the use of specific details.

As the chemical penetrated the soil the poisoned beetle grubs crawled out on the ground, where they remained for some time before they died, attractive to insect-eating birds. Dead and dying insects of various species were conspicuous for about two weeks after the treatment. The effect on the bird populations could easily have been foretold. Brown thrashers, starlings, meadowlarks, grackles, and pheasants were virtually wiped out. Robins were "almost annihilated," according to the biologists' report. Dead earthworms had been seen in numbers after a gentle rain; probably the robins had fed on the poisoned worms. For other birds, too, the once beneficial rain had been changed, through the evil power of the poison introduced into their world, into an agent of destruction. Birds seen drinking and bathing in puddles left by rain a few days after the spraying were inevitably doomed.

—RACHEL CARSON, *The Silent Spring*

The paragraph uses specific, visual details to produce an emotional reaction against pollution. The results of the spraying are shown, not talked about.

HUMAN INTEREST

A strong element of human interest is particularly effective in arousing the sympathy and support of a reader. This process requires an arrangement of details that draws the reader into an action or time-sequence. An anecdote may be used, as in the next example.

At the recent bienniel symposium [of the National Security Industrial Association], the theme was "Research and Development in the 1970s." To my not unalloyed pleasure, I was invited to participate as one of the seventeen speakers and assigned the topic "Planning for the Socio-Economic Environment." Naturally I could make the usual speculations about why I was thus "co-opted." I doubt that they expected to pick my brains for any profitable ideas. But it is useful for feeders at the public trough to present an image of wide-ranging discussion. It is comfortable to be able to say, "You see? these far-outniks *are* impractical." And business meetings are dull and I am notoriously stimulating. But the letter of invitation from Henri Busignies of ITT, the chairman of the symposium committee, said only, "Your accomplishments throughout your distinguished career eminently qualify you to speak with authority on the subject."

What is an intellectual man to do in such a case? I agree with the Gandhian principle, always cooperate within the limits of honor, truth, and justice. But how to co-operate with the military industrial club! during the Vietnam war 1967! It was certainly not the time to reason about basic premises, as is my usual approach, so I decided simply to confront them and soberly tell them off.

—PAUL GOODMAN, "A Causerie at the Military-Industrial"

By the time a reader comes to the end of this anecdote, his curiosity is aroused, and he is inclined to support Goodman's side of the argument.

The emotional impact of this technique can be raised through the use of direct conversation and visual description, as in the following account of a mass arrest in San Francisco.

As soon as the prisoners got off the buses that had brought them to Santa Rita, they were forced to lie on their stomachs, their heads turned to the left, for two-and-one-half hours while the sheriff's deputies alternatively threatened and assaulted them.

"Any of you creeps got a camera, put it out in front of your head," shouted a guard. "We find a camera later and we smash it and your head at the same time."

"Don't none of you move," yelled another. "We shoot to kill here."

"You think this is cold, creeps?" one asked the shirt-sleeved prisoners as the fog rolled in and darkness approached. "It really gets cold in a couple of hours. We'll leave you out here to freeze to death, maybe that will teach you to stay out of Berkeley."

After being searched and sometimes beaten, fingerprints were taken, one guard telling the prisoners, "Hell, we're going to keep track of you troublemakers. We're going to enforce the McCarran Act soon and put all you troublemakers in concentration camps."

—*The New Republic*, "Support Your Local Police"

Through the use of direct conversation and sharp detail, the author of this passage helps the reader to experience the frustration and outrage of the victims. The author himself seems neither to exaggerate nor to editorialize; he lets his facts do the talking.

The use of an anecdote is a good way to strengthen the human interest in an essay, but a similar effect can be achieved through the use of ideas alone. Instead of having a reader identify himself with a person in the essay (either yourself or someone you describe), you can have him participate in the intellectual process of developing a conclusion—a process that can in itself be an emotional experience.

The American people have also become more and more accustomed to militarism, to uniforms, to the cult of the gun, and to the violence of combat. Whole generations have been brought up on war news and wartime propaganda; the few years of peace since 1939 have seen a steady stream of war novels, war movies, comic strips, and television programs with war or military settings. To many Americans, military training, expeditionary service, and warfare are merely extensions of the entertainment and games of childhood. Even the weaponry and hardware they use at war are similar to the highly realistic toys of their youth. Soldiering loses appeal for some of the relatively few who experience the blood, terror, and filth of battle; for many, however, including far too many senior professional officers, war and combat are an exciting adventure, a competitive game, and an escape from the dull routines of peacetime.

—DAVID M. SHOUP, "The New American Militarism"

Most readers would accept the statement that generations of Americans have been reared on images of war. From this idea, General Shoup builds to the conclusion that war itself, for many of us, is merely an extension of childhood games. The uncontroversial beginning of the paragraph lures the reader into a progression of ideas leading to a conclusion that he might otherwise have rejected automatically.

THE APPEAL TO SPECIFIC EMOTIONS

By choosing your details carefully, you should be able to arouse specific emotions in a reader. To do so, consider first the result you want to achieve (the abolishment of an abuse, the forwarding of a worthy cause) and then the specific emotions that should encourage a reader to support it (anger, admiration). In the process, remember that the emotion you want to arouse is not your own, but that of your reader. You may share it, but do not *say* so. Do not say, for example, that something is infuriating and hope that your reader will agree. *Show* how something is infuriating, and let your reader supply the adjectives. Use specific details or anecdotes, and let *them* produce the emotional impact.

The next example is intended to arouse the emotion of anger, and the author depends on specific details to convey his attitude.

The New York Telephone Company is also a monopoly. For that special status the company gives consumers no dial tones, wrong numbers, busy signals for information operators, pay phones that don't function and don't return your dime, and exaggerated bills. It also demands cash deposits from poor people, cooperates with the FBI in illegal taps on private citizens, spends millions each year for newspaper ads and public relations, doesn't answer letters of complaint, and bills customers for wrong numbers. The only stockholder in the New York Telephone Company is AT&T, one of the biggest Vietnam war contractors. Last year, despite deteriorating local service, the telephone company paid AT&T $202.7 million in dividends. In February of this year the telephone company asked the PSC to approve a new 29 per cent rate increase.

—JACK NEWFIELD, "A Populist Manifesto"

Another technique of arousing the emotion of anger is to let the opposition hang itself. In the next example, a military psychiatrist is quoted; then his statement is commented upon.

The basic training period was, therefore, not one of gradual inculcation of the Army mores but one of intensive shock treatment. The new recruit, a lone individual, is helplessly insecure in the bewildering newness and complexity of his environment. Also he is a man; he must show that he is tough enough to "take it.". . . With personal insecurity on the one hand and the motivation to "see it through" on the other he is malleable to the discipline, which consists of a fatiguing physical ordeal and continued repetition of acts until they become semi-automatic, in an atmosphere dominated by fear. . . .

Some of the elements of this process bear remarkable resemblance to the techniques of "brain washing" as reported from prisoner-of-war camps. The fact that our military is willing to exploit the psychological helplessness of the new soldier in this manner is an indictment, not only of the draft, but of the entire war system.

—AMERICAN FRIENDS SERIVCE COMMITTEE, *The Draft?*

By exposing the way the Army conceals its motives from the recruits, the authors intend to direct our anger against the entire military establishment.

In the next paragraph, the positive emotion of tolerance is encouraged through the example of a kindly man.

If we had to vote right now for the man of the year, our choice would be Andy Barker, mayor of Love Valley, a tiny town in North Carolina with a total population of seventy-four. Love Valley was the appropriately named scene last month of a three-day rock festival that attracted 75,000 young people. Mayor Barker handled the event with the kind of aplomb, friendliness, and wisdom that is badly needed at a time when too many people seem eager to connect their prejudices to their tempers and to believe the worst of one another. . . .

"Aren't you offended by the boys' beards?" a reporter asked him.

"My grandfather wore a beard and he thought that men who shaved were trying to imitate women."

The reporter persisted. "What about long hair on boys?"

"Our Lord wore long hair," Mr. Barker replied. "More recently, so did George Washington and Thomas Jefferson."

—NORMAN COUSINS, "All Hail Andy Barker"

Positive emotions may also be aroused in a reader through the description of an idea. The next example supports an Oriental concept of leisure as opposed to an American attitude of aggressiveness.

Sometimes a prophetic vision comes to me, a beautiful vision of a millennium when Manhattan will go slow, and when the American "go-getter" will become an Oriental loafer. American gentlemen will float in skirts and slippers and amble on the sidewalks of Broadway with their hands in their pockets, if not with both hands stuck in their sleeves in the Chinese fashion. Policemen will exchange a word of greeting with the slow-devil at the crossings, and the drivers themselves will stop and accost each other and inquire after their grandmothers' health in the midst of traffic. Some one will be brushing his teeth outside his shopfront, talking the while placidly with his neighbors, and once in a while, an absent-minded scholar will sail by with a limp volume rolled up and tucked away in his sleeve. Lunch counters will be abolished, and people will be lolling and lounging in soft, low armchairs in an Automat. . . . It is too bad that there is no hope of this kind of a millennium on Manhattan ever being realized. There might be so many more perfect idle afternoons.

—LIN YUTANG, *The Importance of Living*

When you use the appeal to emotion, whether it involves an abstract idea or a situation, the crucial point is always to consider the effect you want your discussion to have on your reader. By using specific details and by adding an element of human interest, you can subtly lead him to react in the way you want.

Never tell the reader, show him: this is one of the oldest maxims for writers—and one of the wisest.

THE ETHICAL APPEAL

CHAPTER 5

The ethical appeal is based on the principle that a writer who is respected by his readers will have a better chance of influencing them than someone who is not. The writer has an advantage if his readers already know his good reputation, but such outside information is not at all necessary. An ethical appeal can emerge from the discussion itself, and it works best when it evolves naturally from what is said.

The best general approach to use, as with the appeal to emotion, is that of demonstrating the qualities you want your reader to notice rather than telling him about them. Do not *say* that you are a staunch seeker of truth or a champion of justice; let these virtues become apparent in your writing. But be sure that the virtues *are* apparent. Sometimes it is not enough to *be* a certain kind of person; you must also *show* that you are.

Although no writer should try to project a false image of himself, there are certain qualities in most of us (one hopes) that encourage the respect of a reader. Four of these qualities —objectivity, reasonableness, courage, and humanity—appear in the next example. Taken together, they produce the image of a man you can like and trust—the image of a plaindealer.

I think Man's gradual, creeping contamination of the planet, his sending up of dust into the air, his strontium additive in our bones, his discharge of industrial poisons into rivers that once flowed clear, his mixing of chemicals with fog on the east wind add up to a fantasy of such grotesque proportions as to make everything said on the subject seem pale and anemic by contrast. I hold one share in the corporate earth and am uneasy about the management. Dr. [Willard F.] Libby said there is new evidence that the amount of strontium reaching the body from topsoil impregnated by fallout is "considerably less than the seventy per cent of the topsoil concentration originally estimated." Perhaps we should all feel elated at this, but I don't. The correct amount of strontium with which to impregnate the topsoil is *no* strontium. To rely on "tolerances" when you get into the matter of strontium 90, with three sovereign bomb testers already testing, independently of one another, and about fifty potential bomb testers ready to enter the stratosphere with their contraptions, is to talk with unwarranted complacency. I belong to a small, unconventional school that believes that *no* rat poison is the correct amount to spread in the kitchen where children and puppies can get at it. I believe that *no* chemical waste is the correct amount to discharge into the fresh rivers of the world, and I believe that if there is a way to trap the fumes from factory chimneys, it should be against the law to set these deadly fumes adrift where they can mingle with fog and, given the right conditions, suddenly turn an area into another Donora, Pa.

5
_____
THE ETHICAL APPEAL
67

—E. B. WHITE, *The Points of My Compass*

The four basic qualities of the plaindealer image that emerge from this passage are:

Objectivity
The author is not blinded by his anger or personal prejudices.

Reasonableness
Instead of ad hominem charges or unsup-

ported generalizations, he gives specific details and then proceeds to his conclusion with clear, simple logic.

Courage

He is not afraid to defend his opinions against the Goliaths of this world.

Humanity

He protests the selfish interests of industries and nations, and wants to make the world a better place for mankind to live in.

In your own ethical appeal, try to project one or more of these qualities.

OBJECTIVITY

One of the best ways to convey an image of objectivity is to develop a tone of urbanity, or civilized, polished courtesy. Show that you are not blinded by the passions of any momentary crisis, but are able to depend on the wisdom of the past to clarify your views of the present. For example, illustrate a point with a reference from history.

There was a time, and it was only yesterday, when the United States could and did stand aloof. In the days of our national youth Washington warned against "entangling alliances," John Adams spoke of that "system of neutrality and impartiality" which was to serve us long and well, and Jefferson enumerated among our blessings that we were "kindly separated by nature and a wide ocean from the exterminating havoc of one quarter of the globe." But those days are gone forever. They ended when the First World War began just forty years ago. The youngest Republic is now the oldest, and if life begins at forty, the circumstances of middle age are nonetheless hard and in many ways disappointing.

—ADLAI E. STEVENSON, *Call to Greatness*

Quote or refer to the Bible or a well-known literary work.

It is one of the drawbacks to asceticism that it sees no harm in pleasures other than those of sense, and yet, in fact, not only the best pleasures, but also the very worst, are purely mental. Consider the pleasures of Milton's Satan when he contemplates the harm that he could do to man. As Milton makes him say:

> The mind is its own place, and of itself
> Can make a hell of heaven, a heaven of hell.

—BERTRAND RUSSELL, *Unpopular Essays*

Another way to reinforce an image of objectivity is to insert a touch of humor or irony into your discussion. Anyone who can laugh—especially at himself—shows that he has not lost his head.

OK, I have just finished another book. . . .
You would think that once an author finished writing a book, he can knock the ashes out of his pipe, take a shower, lie back on his hammock, and rake in (or wonder where are) his royalties.
Not true. Once he's laid aside his pen, the author becomes salesman, pitchman, barker, shill, medicine man, who shows up all over the dials to

convince you that if you read his book, your life will be enriched. And so will he.

—GOODMAN ACE, "The Finger, Having Writ, Starts Running"

You can also reinforce your quality of objectivity by presenting an emotionally charged or overly familiar situation from a different perspective, as in the following discussion of racial prejudice.

It seems to me when I watch Americans in Europe that what they don't know about Europeans is what they don't know about me. They were not trying to be nasty to the French girl, rude to the French waiter. They did not know that they hurt their feelings; they didn't have any sense that this particular man and woman were human beings. They walked over them with the same sort of bland ignorance and condescension, the charm and cheerfulness, with which they had patted me on the head and which made them upset when I was upset.

—JAMES BALDWIN, "The American Dream and the American Negro"

REASONABLENESS

As Chapter 3 suggests, it is important to see both sides of every argument; it is equally important to make sure that your reader *knows* you see both sides and are therefore a reasonable person. You may, for example, concede a minor point from time to time—before establishing your own main point more firmly.

I wish I could like submarines, for then I might

find them beautiful, but they are designed for destruction, and while they may explore and chart the sea bottom, and draw new trade lines under the Arctic ice, their main purpose is threat. And I remember too well crossing the Atlantic on a troop ship and knowing that somewhere on the way the dark things lurked searching for us with their single-stalk eyes. Somehow the light goes bleak for me when I see them and remember burned men pulled from the oil-slicked sea. And now submarines are armed with mass murder, our silly, only way of deterring mass murder.

—JOHN STEINBECK, *Travels with Charley*

You may admit the validity of other approaches to a problem.

I certainly would not suggest that the system of symbols and metaphors which I have outlined above is the only frame of reference.... Without depreciating the importance of these and other considerations, however, I do suggest that...

—ROLAND MUSHAT FRYE, "Swift's Yahoo and the Christian Symbols for Sin"

Or you may acknowledge an objection and then qualify your own conclusions.

I do not say that a clear line can be drawn between them; criticism does not hope to be mathematically exact. But...

—PERCY LUBBOCK, *The Craft of Fiction*

Whenever you point out the possible validity of another opinion and the possible weakness of one of your own, you strengthen your image of fairness. Avoid giving *too* much weight to other positions, however; you do not want to appear spineless or indecisive.

Another way to reinforce an image of reasonableness is to make a reader aware of your qualities of openness and honesty.

Retrospects at the ends of books often suffer from one or the other of two common flaws. There is on the one hand the retrospect in name only. Far from being a detached examination of the course and movement of his thought, it is continually in the writer's mind as he composes his work. It is a brooding and directive omnipresence determining, all along, the ways in which the writer's mind shall tread. The retrospect that will here follow avoids such artificiality not through any particular virtue of mine, but simply because the preceding content of this book was almost complete as it here appears before I thought of composing a retrospective conclusion for it. . . .

—J. H. HEXTER, *Reappraisals in History*

A good way to underscore the quality of reasonableness is to remind your reader, always by subtle means, that you are a clear thinker and that you develop arguments logically. You must carefully consider your use of directional signals and the various degrees of strength they may be given. The following sentences provide a choice of increasingly strong directional signals.

This advantage may be compared with another that . . .

Although it is a definite advantage, there is another one that . . .

I have shown the advantages that occur in this situation; I would now like to suggest that . . .

Before continuing with this argument, we should pause for a moment to summarize the major points that have already been made. First . . .

A subtle way to emphasize your use of logical argument is to develop a minor point or to slip into a digression, and then, after finishing, to point out what you have done.

It is here, at last, that we rejoin the main thread of our argument. . . .

—HUGH SYKES DAVIES, "Irony and the English Tongue"

This technique should be used sparingly, however. Even if minor points or digressions add substantially to the main argument (and they always should), too many of them can create an impression of aimlessness.

COURAGE

This quality of the plaindealer image is demonstrated by standing up for your own opinions. In the process, avoid the extremes of arrogance on the one hand and needless apology on the other. Present your case politely, but with direction.

The introduction of color was, I think, one of the great disasters in the development of television technology. It was so expensive simply to transmit tints at all—just to get red and green into the home

—that enormous expense went into this tour de force and very little energy, ingenuity, or money was left over to produce a refined and high quality black and white image. In a sense, this is partly a personal prejudice against color. I can't think of a really good film which has ever been made in color, or at least in which the color has been anything more than just an adventitious aspect of the product. Any serious work of documentary or fictional art in the visual form has almost always been in black and white; and I would personally have liked to see at least half the effort that went into color put into improving the quality of the black and white image and into making the screen larger and the grain of the image finer.

—JONATHAN MILLER, "TV Guide"

Courage can also be demonstrated by criticizing those whom you consider weak-willed, or by praising those who are not.

What is this silence that has fallen on the leadership of the university—presidents, deans, boards of trustees and regents alike? The leaders of the religious community have spoken out boldly enough —heads of great theological seminaries, distinguished theologians and clergymen. The scientific community has taken a strong stand on the moral issues of the war and of nuclear weapons, Nobel Prize winners, heads of great scientific organizations. The rank and file of the academic community, teachers, scholars, students, have seen that here are moral issues that must be faced, and have wrestled with them. But from Cambridge to Berkeley, from Madison to Baton Rouge, not a single president of a great university has taken a public stand on what is the greatest moral issue of our time.

—HENRY STEELE COMMAGER, "The University As Employment Agency"

HUMANITY

One way to project this last quality of the plaindealer image is to refer to yourself directly. The technique can be moving and effective, as long as it does not suggest egotism.

We should never forget that everything Adolf Hitler did in Germany was "legal" and everything the Hungarian freedom fighters did in Hungary was "illegal." It was "illegal" to aid and comfort a Jew in Hitler's Germany. Even so, I am sure that, had I lived in Germany at the time, I would have aided and comforted my Jewish brothers. If today I lived in a Communist country where certain principles dear to the Christian faith are suppressed, I would openly advocate disobeying that country's anti-religious laws.

—MARTIN LUTHER KING, JR., *Why We Can't Wait*

Unless your name has the lustre of Dr. King's, pointing out a virtue of your own may be taken for vanity. It may be advisable, therefore, to *demonstrate* your virtue by strongly supporting a humane ideal.

In the next decades of this country, Americans will be called upon to choose between three fundamentally different options concerning the future course of our society: whether to attempt to turn the clock back so as to "re-create" a bygone society in which our modern alienations did not yet exist, whether to "continue" the present triumphant march of a technological process which has created these same alienations, or whether to begin to define a new vision of a society whose values transcend technology. The first two choices would lead, I believe, to regression or stagnation; only by beginning now to articulate a vision of society in which technology is used for truly human purposes can we create a nation of individuals, a society that *merits* the commitment of its citizens. Yet such a redefinition of purpose has not been forthcoming, and social and political thought in America continues to be dominated by those who would have us regress to the past or those who would merely have us continue our present drift. What is it that prevents our imagining a society radically better than and different from our own?

—KENNETH KENISTON, *The Uncommitted: Alienated Youth in American Society*

Or praise humanity in others and attack those who lack it.

Youthful dissenters are not experts in these matters. But when they see all the wonders of nature being ruined they ask, "What natural law gives the Establishment the right to ruin the rivers, the lakes, the ocean, the beaches, and even the air?"

And if one tells them that the important thing is making money and increasing the Gross National Product they turn away in disgust.

Their protest is not only against what the Establishment is doing to the earth but against the callous attitude of those who claim the God-given right to wreak that damage on the nation without rectifying the wrong.

—WILLIAM O. DOUGLAS, *Points of Rebellion*

In consciously developing the characteristics of objectivity, reasonableness, courage, and humanity in your writing, be careful not to advertise what you are doing. Always keep your argument in the foreground and yourself in the background. A plaindealer never gives the appearance of being self-conscious.

CHAPTER 6 STYLE

Style, or the *manner of writing*, cannot be separated from the content of an essay, nor can it be studied in isolation. The best way to develop a good prose style is to concentrate more on what you have to say than on how you say it.

CLARITY

The essence of good style is clarity. You must be constantly on your guard to avoid the easy but meaningless words and phrases that make up the better part of everyday speech and writing. Take the word *fact*, for example. Often it is used to introduce an idea (the fact that something is so) or to slide from one idea to another (something is due to the fact that). But the word is rarely used to mean *fact*; usually it means *opinion* (the fact that the wine is too dry). When you write *fact* and mean *opinion*, you are not thinking of what your words actually mean.

Sometimes writers intentionally use words to deceive or to mislead, but most people are not consciously dishonest in their choice of words. They are only guilty of wanting to sound sophisticated, or literary, or scientific—of wanting to sound important.

In studying the motivation factors that operate in various pre-adult male groups, psychologists have discovered certain inherent characteristics which, although they are made manifest in different reaction patterns, have a tendency to be typical of adolescents.

Which is to say, "Boys will be boys."

Some people fear that if they write simply they will appear simple-minded as well. But it is the subject matter of a piece of writing that determines its intellectual level, not the length of its sentences or the number of its sesquipedalian words. Indeed, when your subject matter is complex, you have all the greater need to write simply in order to be understood.

Economy

One of the secrets of good style is economy. If you can express an idea in half as many words, do so.

This is the man who recognized the fact that the gun wasn't loaded.

This man knew the gun was empty.

Make the words you use earn their keep. Instead of a vague noun qualified by an adjective (the small stone) use a precise noun (the pebble). Instead of a colorless verb qualified by adverbs (the river went along very quickly), use a strong verb (the river surged).

Very, little, quite, for the most part, perhaps, really, more or less, rather—these and other common qualifiers can drain the life out of a paragraph. Sometimes they are necessary, but try to choose nouns and verbs strong enough to stand alone.

Avoid using wordy phrases when they can be replaced by adequate verbs (make contact with—meet; is of the opinion that—believes; the reason I am going is that—I am going because). Avoid phrases that introduce qualifications where none are needed (for the most part, to a certain extent, up to a point, in many cases). Avoid inflated phrases that do not affect the sense of what you are saying (as far as such-and-such is concerned, in terms of, in view of the fact that).

Abstract Nouns

The excessive use of abstract nouns (*aspect, condition, concept, situation, function, picture, character*) can make your writing obtuse; and when they are piled on top of one another (the aspect of a condition, the picture of a situation, the character of a function), the result can become incomprehensible. Is a condition part of an aspect, or is an aspect part of a condition? Can the character of a situation have functions?

Such confusion increases when you use nouns that have a literal as well as an abstract or figurative meaning (*field, area, head, branch, picture*). You can properly use either meaning (a green field; the field of international affairs), but watch out for such absurdities as *the head of a foreign branch* or *the field of mountain climbing.*

When you use abstract nouns, know exactly what they mean. And make sure that your reader does too.

Passive Verbs

Choose active verbs wherever possible; passive verbs tend to obscure their sources. *The film is supposed to be hilarious* does not say who does the supposing. The sentence would be more persuasive if it named its authorities: *The reviewers of both the* Los Angeles Times *and the* Saturday Review *found the film hilarious.*

The Verb To Be

The verb *to be*, although an indispensable part of the language, is often overworked.

America's new military power is the cause of the new curse. There is a form of Parkinson's Law in operation here. The greater the power is seen to be, the more it is extolled by the men who are associated with it. They are able to find needs, real or sophistical, for it to be used.

The original version of this passage reads

The new curse has come with America's new military power. A form of Parkinson's Law operates here. The greater the power, the more the men who associate with it, extoll it and find needs, real or sophistical, for its use. . . .

—ERIC SEVAREID, "The American Dream"

You can usually remove an excess of *to be* forms by compression, by the substitution of stronger and more precise verbs, or by simple omission; the hard part is to notice when you are overworking them.

You should also avoid overworking common substitutes for *to be* (*seem, arise, become, exist, involve, concern, deal with, relate to*).

It Is Constructions

Idioms consisting of the anticipatory *it* or *there* plus a form of the verb *to be* (it is useful, it was raining, there is hope) should be used sparingly, especially at the beginning of a sentence. Sometimes these constructions can be used for emphasis (there is a tide in the affairs of men), but their overuse is a sign of flabby prose.

Fatigued Metaphors

Fatigued metaphors and other tired figures of speech (cool as a cucumber, sick to death of, tried and true) blunt the impact of prose. Their presence is irritating and distracting, and your reader may suspect that your ideas are also fatigued. Avoid using any metaphor or figure of speech that you suspect of being a cliché. It probably is.

EFFECTIVE QUOTATION

One of the best ways to make your writing interesting and authoritative is to use direct quotation—if you do so correctly and well. To quote correctly, consult *The MLA Style Sheet* (revised edition); to quote well, use the following techniques.

Quote an authority by blending a few words or phrases of the original into your own sentence structure.

> Forest Lawn offers the largest religious painting in the United States, displayed in a building, the Hall of the Crucifixion, specially designed for it. There, for a voluntary contribution of twenty-five cents, the visitor sits comfortably in a large theatre, in one of a "broad sweep of seats, richly upholstered in burgundy, rising tier above tier, matching the splendor of the architecture," and watches the three-thousand-pound curtain open on Jesus at Calvary, forty-five feet high and 195 feet long. . . .
>
> —PAUL JACOBS, "The Most Cheerful Graveyard in the World"

This technique may also be used to lead into a quotation of several lines, one that is long enough to indent and single-space.

> Mandeville, a tavern character whose malice sharpened his wit, was especially qualified to expose weaknesses of what he disliked. He disliked the *Characteristics* of the third Earl of Shaftesbury, which presented a system of ethics not only contrary to his own, but, he maintained, contrary to the teachings of "the generality of moralists and philosophers" up to that time. Shaftesbury, he said,
>
> > imagines that men without any trouble or violence upon themselves may be naturally virtuous. He seems to require and expect goodness in his species, as we do a sweet taste in grapes and China oranges, of which, if any of them are sour, we boldly pronounce that they are not come to that perfection their nature is capable of. . . .
>
> —LOUIS I. BREDVOLD, "The Gloom of the Tory Satirists"

If you consider a quotation to be particularly important, you may want to use a formal introduction—one that draws attention to the quotation *as* a quotation.

In his Mellon lectures in 1960 Mr. Lewis made the differentiation simply and accurately:

> Walpole was not a bibliophile; he scorned the mysteries of what is today called bibliography and he had little curiosity about textual variants. He bought a few books for their bindings and rarity and for their association with early owners, but not many. He bought his books to read.
>
> —ALLEN T. HAZEN, "The Earlier Owners of Walpole's Books"

If a quotation is long, use a follow-up passage (like the next one) to make sure that your reader did not miss the main point. The Hazen passage just quoted continues:

> Therefore, although Walpole is recorded by Fletcher and De Ricci as a book collector, we can more properly say that he collected many memorable oddities other than books at Strawberry Hill, but that his books were selected for reading and study, to be annotated and referred to, to form the materials for his understanding and recording of the life of his time. . . .
>
> —ALLEN T. HAZEN, "The Earlier Owners of Walpole's Books"

Be sure that your authority is always named *before* you quote him. A mystery quotation— one that appears without prior identification—

inevitably works against you. A reader resents having his curiosity aroused for no good purpose. Footnoting the source or mentioning it later on in your discussion is no help. If the author is worth quoting, he is worth introducing first.

REVISION

Writing effectively requires extensive revision. As you revise, ask yourself the following questions:

Is my thesis clear?

Do all my paragraphs hold together as units? Can I identify all my topic sentences or justify their absence?

Are my directional signals clear?

Can I throw out any paragraphs without damaging my thesis?

Is my introduction short enough? Should an attention-getting opening be used? Should I begin with the second paragraph?

Is the ending of my essay effective? Is it short enough?

Are there any other kinds of argument I can use effectively in proving my thesis?

Do I refute the obvious objections to my thesis?

What emotional responses do I want my

reader to have? Will my discussion produce them?

Do I *show* the reader what to think or just *tell* him?

What image of myself do I present? Does my writing make me appear objective, reasonable, courageous, humane?

Can I omit some of my passive verbs? Or some of the *to be* constructions? Can I make my verbs stronger and my abstract nouns clearer? Can I omit unnecessary *it is* constructions and fatigued metaphors?

Can I condense my discussion anywhere without losing clarity?

If, in the process of revising, your manuscript becomes too messy to read easily, rewrite or retype it and continue your work. Save all your old drafts, however; you may decide later that a rejected part of one is salvageable. If you find yourself going around in circles, put your draft aside and come back to it a day (or even an hour) later.

Imagine yourself reading your paper aloud to a group of friends. Is there anything that would embarrass you? Do you know what you are talking about? Are you ever pompous, coy, or pretentious?

Do not be discouraged if you take a long time making your discussion come out right. Hard work is a prerequisite of clear, persuasive prose.

SOURCES OF EXAMPLES

Ace, Goodman 69–70

"Top of My Head: The Finger Having Writ, Starts Running," in Saturday Review, 29 August 1970.

American Friends Service Committee 62

The Draft? A Report Prepared for the Peace Education Division of the AFSC. Hill & Wang, 1968.

Baldwin, James 70

"The American Dream and the American Negro," in *The New York Times Magazine,* 7 March 1965.

Baugh, Albert C. 11

"The Renaissance, 1500–1650," *A History of the English Language.* Appleton-Century-Crofts, 2nd ed., 1957.

Bettelheim, Bruno 45

"The Problem of Generations," in *Daedalus,* Winter, 1962.

Bredvold, Louis I. 83

"The Gloom of the Tory Satirists," in *Pope and His Contemporaries: Essays Presented to George Sherburn,* ed. James L. Clifford and Louis A. Landa. Oxford, 1949; reprinted in *Eighteenth-Century English Literature: Modern Essays in Criticism,* ed. James L. Clifford, Galaxy.*

* Reprints refer to paperback editions.

Davies, Hugh Sykes

"Irony and the English Tongue," in *The World of Jonathan Swift*, ed. Brian Vickers. Harvard, 1968.

Douglas, William O.

"The Legions of Dissent," in *Points of Rebellion*. Random House, 1969; reprinted by Vintage.

Feuer, Louis

"Should College Students Grade Their Teachers? The Risk is 'Juvenocracy,'" in *The New York Times Magazine*, 18 September 1966.

Forster, E. M.

"What I Believe," in *Two Cheers for Democracy*. Harcourt Brace Jovanovich, 1951; reprinted by Harvest.

Frye, Roland Mushat

"Swift's Yahoo and the Christian Symbols for Sin," in *Journal of the History of Ideas*, April 1964.

Geltman, Max

"The New Left and the Old Right," in *National Review*, 13 June 1967.

Goodman, Paul

"A Causerie at the Military-Industrial," in *The New York Review of Books*, 23 November 1967; reprinted in *People or Personnel and Like a Conquered Province*, Vintage.

Haagen-Smit, Arie J.   **47**

"The Troubled Outdoors," in *Interactions of Man and His Environment*, ed. Burgess H. Jennings and John E. Murphy. Northwestern, 1966.

Hamilton, Edith   **22**

"The Idea of Tragedy," in *The Greek Way*. Norton, 1948.

Harrington, Michael   **43–44**

"The Statues of Daedalus," in *The Accidental Century*. Macmillan, 1965; reprinted by Pelican.

Hazen, Allen T.   **84**

"The Earlier Owners of Horce Walpole's Books," in *Horace Walpole: Writer, Politician, and Connoisseur*, ed. Warren H. Smith. Yale, 1967.

Hersey, John   **37**

Hiroshima. Knopf, 1946; reprinted by Bantam.

Hexter, J. H.   **72**

"Personal Retrospect and Postscript," in *Reappraisals in History: New Views on History and Society in Early Modern Europe*. Northwestern, 1961; reprinted by Harper Torchbooks.

Hook, Sidney   **13–14**

"A Program for Education," in *Education for Modern Man: A New Perspective*. Knopf, new enlarged ed., 1963.

Lubbock, Percy   **71**

The Craft of Fiction. Scribner's, 1921; reprinted by Compass.

May, Rollo   **41–42**

"Antidotes for the New Puritanism," in *Saturday Review*, 26 March 1966; reprinted in a revised form in *Love and Will*, Norton, 1969.

Milford, Nancy   **26–27**

Zelda. Harper & Row, 1970; reprinted by Avon.

Miller, Jonathan   **73–74**

"TV Guide," in *The New York Review of Books*, 7 October 1971.

Mumford, Lewis   **39–40**

"The Highway and the City," in *The Highway and the City.* Harcourt Brace Jovanovich, 1962.

The New Republic   **58–59**

"Support Your Local Police," in *The New Republic*, 21 June 1969.

Newfield, Jack   **61**

"A Populist Manifesto: The Making of the New Majority," in *New York* Magazine, 19 July 1971.

Nicolson, Marjorie Hope   **12**

"The Literary Heritage," in *Mountain Gloom and Mountain Glory: The Development of the Aesthetics of the Infinite.* Cornell, 1959; reprinted by Norton.

Orwell, George   38

"Politics and the English Language," in *Shooting an Elephant and Other Essays*. Harcourt Brace, 1950; reprinted in *A Collection of Essays by George Orwell*, Anchor.

Piel, Gerard   42–43

Science in the Cause of Man. Knopf, 2nd ed., 1962.

Riesman, David   45

"Where is the College Generation Headed?" in *Atlantic Monthly*, April 1961.

Rossiter, Clinton   46

"The Conservative Tradition," in *Conservatism in America: The Thankless Persuasion*. Vintage, 2nd ed. rev., 1962.

Russell, Bertrand   69

"Ideas That Have Harmed Mankind," in *Unpopular Essays*. Simon & Schuster, 1950.

Schlesinger, Arthur M., Jr.   7

"Invasion of Europe, Family Style," in *The New York Times Magazine*, 11 August 1957; reprinted in *The Politics of Hope*, Houghton Mifflin, 1963.

Sevareid, Eric   81

"The American Dream," in *Look* Magazine, 9 July 1968.

Shoup, David M.   59–60

"The New American Militarism," in *Atlantic Monthly*, April 1969.

Steinbeck, John 70–71

Travels with Charley in Search of America. Viking, 1962; reprinted by Compass, Bantam.

Stevenson, Adlai E. 68–69

Call to Greatness. Harper & Row, 1954.

Thurber, James 26

"Miracle Men," in *The Years with Ross.* Little Brown, 1959; reprinted by Signet.

Ward, Barbara 49

"Hindsight and Foresight in the World Economy," in *Columbia Forum*, Spring 1969.

Wheelwright, Philip 41

A Critical Introduction to Ethics. Odyssey, 3rd ed., 1959.

White, E. B. 66–67

The Points of My Compass: Letters from the East, the West, the North, the South. Harper & Row 1962.

Whyte, William H., Jr. 18–19

"The Decline of the Protestant Ethic," in *The Organization Man.* Simon & Schuster, 1956; reprinted by Anchor.

Wiener, Norbert 24–25

"Some Moral and Technical Consequences of Automation," in *Science*, 6 May 1960.

Williams, Raymond   43

"Prelude to Alienation," in *Dissent*, Summer, 1964.

Woodring, Paul   3

"Eros on the Campus," in *The Higher Learning in America*. McGraw Hill, 1968.

Yutang, Lin   63–64

"Three American Vices," in *The Importance of Living*. John Day, 1937.

INDEX

A

Abstract nouns, misuse of, 80
Ace, Goodman, quoted, 69–70
Admiration, arousing emotions of, 60–1, 62–3
Ad populum, logical fallacy, 36
Aesop, fables of, as source of aphorisms, 50
Alice in Wonderland, mentioned by Marchette Chute, 28, 31
Allusion, literary, technique of beginning with a, 28
Although-because method of limiting a thesis, 15
American Friends Servcie Committee, quoted, 62
American society, future course of, discussed by Kenneth Keniston, 75–6
American stock, discussed by Max Lerner, 51–2
Analogies, use of, in argument, 46–9
Anecdote
    beginning with, 26
    use of in arousing emotions, 57–8, 59
Anger, arousing emotions of, 60–2
Aphorisms, use of, in argument, 49–50
Apologetic beginning, 29
Appeal to emotion, *see* Emotion, appeal to
Appeal to reason, *see* Reason, appeal to
Argument
    acknowledging weaknesses in, 37
    any can be challenged, 36
    circular, 35
    developing logically, to show reasonableness, 72
    finding an, 52–3
    kinds of, 38–51
    specific kinds not used in isolation, 51
    two kinds of logic used in all, 34
    use of, 51–3
Aristotle
    as a standard authority, 41
    his definition of rhetoric, Preface

Army, basic training in, discussed by AFSC, 62
Arrest, mass, in San Francisco, discussed by *The New Republic*, 58–9
Artistic approach, 29
Asceticism, discussed by Bertrand Russell, 69
Aspect, misuse of, 80
Atlantic citadel, discussed by Barbara Ward, 49
Authority, kind of argument, 41–2
Authority, standard, see standard authority
Author's qualifications, drawing attention to, 24
Automation, discussed by Norbert Wiener, 24–5

B

Baldwin, James, quoted, 70
Barker, Andy, praised by Norman Cousins, 62–3
Basic training, discussed by AFSC, 62
Baugh, Albert C., quoted, 11
Begging the question, logical fallacy, 35–6
Beginnings, 22–30
    beginning with thesis sentence first, 29–30
    elements of, 22
    kinds of
        anecdote, 26
        bon mot, 28
        definition, 23–4
        discovery, 25–6
        literary allusion, 28
        mystery, 26-7
        personal history, 24–5
        pertinent quotation, 27–8
    merging of elements of, 23
    unwise approaches, 28–9
Berkeley
    mass arrest in, discussed by *The New Republic*, 58–9
    students at, discussed by Max Geltman, 27–8
Bettelheim, Bruno, quoted, 45
Bible
    as source of proverbs, 50
    references to, to convey objectivity, 69

Boaz, Franz, cited by Max Lerner, 51
Bon mot, technique of beginning with, 28
Brain-washing, in U.S. Army, discussed by AFSC,
    62
Bread, outlines for essay on, 16–18
Bronowski, J., quoted, 3–4

C

California, University of, discussed by Max Gelt-
    man, 27–8
Carlyle, Thomas, his influence on Marx, discussed
    by Raymond Williams, 43
Carson, Rachel, quoted, 56–7
Cause and effect
    kind of argument, 42–4
    examples of, 52, 53
    refutation of argument based on, 43
Cemetery, Forest Lawn, discussed by Paul Jacobs, 83
Change, result of cultural factors on, discussed by
    Max Lerner, 51–2
Character, misuse of, 80
Chronology, order of, 8
Chummy approach, 29
Chute, Marchette, quoted, 28, 31
Cicero, suggests method of limiting thesis, 14
Circular argument, 35
Clarity, the basic principle of structure, 2
Cleaver, Eldridge, quoted, 44
Clifford, James L., quoted, 37–8
Colleges, obsolete, discussed by Robert M. Hutchins,
    30, 32
Commager, Henry Steele, quoted, 74
Comparisons, 44–9
    examples of, 52, 53
    figurative, 45–6
    refutation of, 44
Complex question, logical fallacy, 36
Concept, misuse of, 80
Conclusions, exaggerated, 38
Condition, misuse of, 80

D

Dramatic emphasis, putting topic sentence last to achieve it, 10

Evidence
  being critical about quality of, 38
  problem of insufficient, 37
Exordium
  definition of, 22
  examples of, 23–8

F

Fact, misuse of, 78
Facts, historical, discussed by Marchette Chute, 28, 31
Fairness, conveying image of, 71
Fallacies, logical, 35–6
Fatigued metaphors, 82
Feuer, Lewis S., quoted, 47–8
Figurative comparisons, 45–6
Fitzgerald, Zelda, discussed by Nancy Milford, 26–7
Flamingoes, mentioned by Marchette Chute, 28, 31
Flour, outline for essay on, 16–18
Forest Lawn cemetery, discussed by Paul Jacobs, 83
Forster, E. M., quoted, 50
For the most part, as qualifer, 79
Frame, method of structuring an essay, 30–1
Franklin, Benjamin, his *Poor Richard's Almanack* as a source of aphorisms, 50
French introduction to sex, discussed by Bruno Bettelheim, 45
French vegetables, discussed by Julia Child, 25
Frye, Roland Mushat, quoted, 71

G

Geltman, Max, quoted, 27–8
Greek tragedy, discussed by Edith Hamilton, 22
Green beans, discussed by Julia Child, 25
Goodman, Paul, quoted, 57–8

H

Haagen-Smit, Arie J., quoted, 47

Invasions of Europe, discussed by Arthur M. Schlesinger, Jr., 7
Isolationism of U.S., discussed by Adlai E. Stevenson, 68–9
It is constructions, misuse of, 82

J

Jacobs, Paul, quoted, 83
Johnson, Samuel, discussed by James L. Clifford, 37–8
Jones, Le Roi, quoted, 23–4

K

Kazin, Alfred, quoted, 10–11
Keniston, Kenneth, quoted, 75–6
Kennedy, John F., quoted, 5–6
King, Martin Luther, Jr., quoted, 75
Kronenberger, Louis, quoted, 28

L

Language, discussed by Albert C. Baugh, 11
Leisure, oriental concept of, discussed by Lin Yutang, 63–4
Lerner, Max, quoted, 51–2
Lewis, Wilmarth S., mentioned by Allen T. Hazen, 84
Libby, Dr. Willard, mentioned by E. B. White, 66–7
Literature, the teaching of one's own, discussed by Alfred Kazin, 11
Literary allusion, technique of beginning with a, 28
Literary reference
example of, 53
use of, in argument, 50–1
Little, as qualifier, 79
Logic, deductive
defined, 34
how it can be questioned, 36

N

Narrative
    definition of, 22
    examples of, 23–8
Nature, seventeenth-century poet's response to,
    discussed by Majorie Hope Nicolson, 12
Nature of a thing
    defined, 38–9
    depends heavily on assertion, 40
    examples of, 52, 53
    refutation of argument based on, 40
Newfield, Jack, quoted, 61
New Left, discussed by Max Geltman, 27–8
New Republic, The, quoted, 58–9
New York City, vision of oriental leisure in,
    discussed by Lin Yutang, 63–4
New Yorker, editor of, discussed by
    James Thurber, 26
New York Telephone Company, discussed by
    by Jack Newfield, 61
Nicolson, Majorie Hope, quoted, 12
Nouns, abstract, misuse of, 80
Nouns, vague, 79

O

Objections to an argument, acknowledging, 71
Objectivity, quality of the plaindealer image
    defined, 67
    how demonstrated, 68–70
    use of a different perspective to convey, 70
    use of humor to convey, 69–70
    use of reference from history to convey, 68
    use of reference to the Bible to convey, 69
    use of urbanity to convey, 68
Open Door Policy, discussed by Eldridge Cleaver, 44
Openness, showing, to convey reasonableness, 71–2
Opinion, use of *fact* to mean, 78
Order, principle of
    defined, 4

different kinds used together, 7
example of, 7
jumbled, 8
list of ordering devices, 6–7
problems of in limiting a thesis, 15–16
Organization Man, discussed by William H. Whyte, Jr., 18–19
Orwell, George, quoted, 38
Outlines
    reason for, 16
    sentence, 17–18
    topic, 16–17
Overly dramatic approach, 29
Overly mechanical approach, 29
Oversimplification, logical fallacy, 35
Oxford English Dictionary, as standard authority, 41

P

Painting of Crucifixion, discussed by Paul Jacobs, 83
Paradise Lost, quoted by Bertrand Russell, 69
Paragraph outline, example of, 17–18
Paragraph, proof, *see* proof paragraph
Paragraph, structure of, *see* proof paragraph
Partition
    definition of, 22
    examples of, 23–8
Passive verbs, misuse of, 81
Perhaps, as qualifier, 79
Personal history, beginning with an example of, 24
Personal relations, discussed by E. M. Forster, 50
Personal testimony, use of, 41–2
Persepctive, different, *see* different perspective
Pertinent quotation, beginning with, 27
Picture, misuse of, 80
Piel, Gerard, quoted, 42–3
Plaindealer image, 66–76
    definition of, 66
    examples of, 66–7, 68–76
    qualities of, 67–8

Politics, discussed by John F. Kennedy, 5–6
Pollution
    discussed by Rachel Carson, 56–7
    discussed by William O. Douglas, 76
    discussed by Arie J. Haagen-Smit, 47
    discussed by E. B. White, 66–7
Poor Richard's Almanack, as source of aphorisms, 50
Post hoc, ergo propter hoc fallacy, 48
Proof, definition of, 2
Proof essay, 2, 12–20
    definition of, 2
    order and subordination in, 12–13
    principles of proof paragraph structure apply
        to, 12
Proof paragraph
    definition of, 2
    standard position of topic sentence in, 2
    structure, models of, 3–4, *passim*
    variation of topic sentence position in, 10–12
Proof structure, 1–20
    definition of, 2
    need for, to write clearly, 2
    variations in
        topic sentence first in the next paragraph, 11
        topic sentence last, 10
        topic sentence second, 11
Protestant Ethic
    discussed by Michael Harrington, 44
    discussed by William H. Whyte, Jr., 18–19
Proverbs, use of in argument, 49–50

Q

Qualifiications, drawing attention to author's, 24
Quality, order of, 6
Quantity, order of, 6
Question, begging the, logical fallacy, 35–6
Quotation
    beginning with a, 27
    blending into your own structure, 83
    effective, 82–5

follow-up summary of, 84
formal introduction of, 84
leading into a, 83
mystery, 84–5

R

Racism
    discussed by James Baldwin, 70
    discussed by Eldridge Cleaver, 44
Rather, as qualifier, 79
Rational appeal, *see* reason, appeal to
Really, as qualifier, 79
Reason, appeal to, 34–53
    combining various kinds of argument in, 51–2
    definition of, 34
    finding arguments for, 52–3
    kinds of argument used in
        authority, 41–2
        cause and effect, 42–4
        comparisons, 44–9
        nature of a thing, 38–40
        proverbs, parables, and literary references, 49–50
    logical fallacies in, 35–6
    psychological foundation of, 34
    use of logic in, 34
Reasonableness, appealing to reader's sense of, 34, 38
Reasonableness, quality of plaindealer image, 70–3
    being open and honest, 71–2
    conceding minor points to show, 70–1
    defined, 67–8
    how demonstrated, 70–3
    use of digressions to show, 73
Rebellions, student
    discussed by Lewis S. Feuer, 47–8
    discussed by Max Geltman, 27–8
Red herring, logical fallacy, 35
References, literary, *see* literary references

Refutation
   definition of, 36–7
   need for, 36
   of arguments based on cause and effect, 43
   of arguments based on comparisons, 44
   of arguments based on metaphors and similes, 46
   of arguments based on the nature of a thing, 40
Relations, personal, discussed by E. M. Forster, 50
Retrospects, discussed by J. H. Hexter, 72
Revision, 85–6
Rhetoric, definition of, Preface
Riesman, David, quoted, 45
Rock festival at Love Valley, discussed by Norman Cousins, 62–3
Ross, Harold, discussed by James Thurber, 26
Rossiter, Clinton, quoted, 46
Russell, Bertrand, quoted, 69

S

San Francisco, mass arrest in, described by *The New Republic*, 58–9
Schlesinger, Arthur M., Jr., quoted, 7
Science, defined by J. Bronowski, 3–4
Science, American, endowment of, discussed by Gerard Piel, 42–3
Self-consciousness, how to avoid, 76
Senators, U.S., discussion of by John F. Kennedy, 5–6
Sentence outlines, *see* outlines
Sentence, thesis, *see* thesis sentence
Sex, French introduction to, discussed by Bruno Bettelheim, 45
Sexual revolution, discussed by Paul Woodring, 3
Shaftesbury, Anthony Ashley Cooper, 3rd Earl of, discussed by Louis I. Bredvold, 83
Shift-of-level ending, 31
Shirtsleeves approach, 29
Shocking topics, preparing for, 10

Testimony, personal, use of, 41–2
There is constructions, misuse of, 82
Thesis
    definition of, 2
    kinds of arguments to support a, 38
    limiting the, 14
    supported by proof paragraphs, 14
Thesis sentence
    beginning with, can be too abrupt, 22
    construction of, 13
    definition of, 2
    variations in position of
        at end of essay, 30
        at end of first paragraph, 25
        at top of the essay, 30
        standard position of, 13
Thing, nature of a, *see* nature of a thing
Thurber, James, quoted, 26
Time, order of, 8
To be, misuse of, 81–2
Topic outline, *see* outlines
Topic sentence
    definition of, 2
    variations in position of
        last in paragraph, 10
        no topic sentence, 12
        second in paragraph, 11
        standard position of, 10
Topic sentences, isolation of, as a check, 18
Training, basic, *see* basic training
Tragedy, discussed by Edith Hamilton, 22
Transportaiton, discussed by Lewis Mumford, 39–40
Truth in writing history, discussed by Marchette Chute, 28, 31

U

Unbelievable topics, preparing for, 10
Urbanity, use of, in conveying objectivity, 68

V

Vegetables, cooking of, discussed by Julia Child, 25
Verbs
    colorless, 79
    passive, misuse of, 81
Very, as qualifier, 79
Vietnam war, silence of university presidents on, discussed by Henry Steele Commager, 74
Visual description, use of in arousing emotions, 58

W

Walpole, Horace, discussed by Allen T. Hazen, 84
Ward, Barbara, quoted, 49
Weaknesses, acknowledging, in argument, 37
Weber, Max, mentioned by Michael Harrington, 43
Webster, in phrase *Webster says*, 41
Wheelwright, Philip, quoted, 41
White, E. B., quoted, 66–7
Whyte, William H., Jr., quoted, 18–19
Wiener, Norbert, quoted, 24–5
Williams, Raymond, quoted, 43
Woodring, Paul, quoted, 3
World economy, discussed by Barbara Ward, 49

Y

Yukawa, Hideki, mentioned by J. Bronowski, 3–4
Yutang, Lin, quoted, 63–4